# Praise for
## *Taming the Drunken Monkey*

"William Mikulas has written a book that provides a wise and delightful guide to living a mindful life ... a helpful, systematic, and very practical guide that presents numerous insights and exercises for personal transformation."

—Nirbhay N. Singh,
editor of the international journal *Mindfulness*

"Whether you are interested in quieting your mind, increasing awareness, reducing attachments, or opening the heart, you will find just what you need as you continue on your path towards awakening."

—Michael Brant DeMaria, PhD,
clinical psychologist and author of *Ever Flowing On*

"This is, undoubtedly, one of the best mind training manuals that has ever been written ... This book can help you cultivate your mind and will improve your life."

—Sompoch Iamsupasit, PhD,
professor at Chulalongkorn University

"For everybody who wants to be aware and mindful, attentive and concentrated ... Bill Mikulas' book is wholeheartedly recommended."

—G.T. Maurits Kwee, PhD,
founder of the Institute for Relational Buddhism and
Karma Transformation

# TAMING
## THE DRUNKEN
### MONKEY

## About the Author

William L. Mikulas, PhD (Pensacola, Florida) is the author of numerous books and articles on interfacing Western psychology and Eastern wisdom and health traditions. He has been a college professor for forty years, during which he earned many awards for teaching, research, and service, and he became Professor Emeritus in 2009. Mikulas has also done lectures, interviews, and workshops around the world on Buddhism and Western psychology.

## To Write to the Author

If you wish to contact the author or would like more information about this book, please write to the author in care of Llewellyn Worldwide, and we will forward your request. Both the author and publisher appreciate hearing from you and learning of your enjoyment of this book and how it has helped you. Llewellyn Worldwide cannot guarantee that every letter written to the author can be answered, but all will be forwarded. Please write to:

William L. Mikulas, PhD
c/o Llewellyn Worldwide
2143 Wooddale Drive
Woodbury, MN 55125-2989

Please enclose a self-addressed stamped envelope for reply,
or $1.00 to cover costs. If outside the USA, enclose
an international postal reply coupon.

# TAMING
# THE DRUNKEN
# MONKEY

The Path to Mindfulness, Meditation,
and Increased Concentration

## WILLIAM L. MIKULAS, PhD

Llewellyn Publications
Woodbury, Minnesota

First Edition
Second Printing, 2014

Book design by Bob Gaul
Cover design by Percolator Graphic Design
Cover image © iStockphoto.com/14192486/Kittisuper
Editing by Laura Graves
Interior image © iStock.com/27722162/Liufuyu

Llewellyn Publications is a registered trademark of Llewellyn Worldwide Ltd.

**Library of Congress Cataloging-in-Publication Data (Pending)**
978-0-7387-3469-9

Llewellyn Worldwide Ltd. does not participate in, endorse, or have any authority or responsibility concerning private business transactions between our authors and the public.

All mail addressed to the author is forwarded, but the publisher cannot, unless specifically instructed by the author, give out an address or phone number.

Any Internet references contained in this work are current at publication time, but the publisher cannot guarantee that a specific location will continue to be maintained. Please refer to the publisher's website for links to authors' websites and other sources.

Llewellyn Publications
A Division of Llewellyn Worldwide Ltd.
2143 Wooddale Drive
Woodbury, MN 55125-2989
www.llewellyn.com

Printed in the United States of America

# Contents

*For Benita, of course*
*a constant gift*

# *Overview*

The mind often acts like a drunken monkey, largely out of control. You will learn how to tame the monkey and thus have a mind that works better. From this book you will learn how to develop and improve three basic behaviors of the mind: concentration, awareness, and flexibility. Developing concentration will help you focus your attention, control your thoughts, and quiet your runaway mind. Developing awareness will help you have broader and clearer awareness of your body, feelings, thoughts, and the world around you. This awareness will lead to more choice, control, and freedom. And developing flexibility will increase creativity and free you from many mental blocks and biases. You will perceive and think more clearly and freely.

The mind is an amazing power tool...that has been turned on and is now running out of control! Although everyone has this power tool, no one was given a manual for how to use it. This book is that instruction manual. The procedures of mental development that you will learn are drawn from around the world and have been well-established in practice and research. This manual is not some trendy theory or popular psychology. Rather, this is the best of world knowledge about how to tame, develop, and free your mind. Some of the procedures have been developed over thousands of years and across very diverse cultures.

The fact that you can understand this introductory section means you can understand the whole book, and you can significantly improve your life with the practices. Learning how to use your mind more effectively is one of the most important things you can do with your life. It will help in work and play, in sports and art, and in your relationships with others. It will reduce stress and increase pleasure, happiness, and peace of mind.

In addition, the mind and brain follow the use-it-or-lose-it principle. Elderly people who actively use their minds, as with games and puzzles, suffer less biological breakdown of the brain, as seen in dementia such as Alzheimer's disease. People who continue to use the mental skills described in this manual stay mentally sharper than those who let these skills gradually decline.

## Concentration

Concentration is the learned ability to keep one's mind focused; it is the opposite of a mind that is wildly jumping around. With concentration you can fully listen to people and clearly hear what they say. Without concentration your mind wanders to other things, and as a result, you often miss something said or you hear it incorrectly. With concentration you can more fully enjoy sights, sounds, tastes, smells, and feelings. Without concentration many of these potential sources of pleasure go unnoticed or unappreciated. Concentration helps you stop and smell the roses.

With further development of concentration, you gain control of the thoughts and memories of the mind. If thoughts or memories arise that cause anxiety, you now have the ability to stop them. Simply trying to suppress undesired thoughts or replace them with desired thoughts does not work very well. Developing concentration is the way to control the contents of the mind. Rather than thoughts controlling you, you control the thoughts. Developing concentration also helps relax and quiet the mind; mental agitation is decreased and peace of mind arises. Quieting the mind decreases stress and increases health. Since the body and mind are totally intertwined, relaxing the mind also helps relax the body.

## Awareness

Developing greater awareness of your body helps in reducing stress and pain, and leads to better understanding of how things such as breathing and nutrition affect your energy, mood, and health. Becoming more aware of your feelings and thoughts—and noticing them earlier and earlier—leads to more control of them. For example, it will be easier to stop getting angry.

Developing greater awareness of the external world will reduce incidents such as car accidents, as well as forgetfulness and the need for double-checking, for example, whether you turned off the burner or locked the door. Becoming more aware of other people will improve your personal and work relationships. To be fully with another person when your mind is concentrated and aware is a wonderful gift that is usually quickly appreciated.

Developing awareness is central to many Western psychotherapies, such as Gestalt therapy and mindfulness-based therapies. Developing awareness facilitates playing musical instruments, playing sports, and exploring one's consciousness and sense of self.

## Flexibility

Mental flexibility will be increased through practices designed to improve your creativity and lateral thinking. Practices include questioning your assumptions, being willing to make mistakes, and thinking in new ways. These practices will usually be playful and fun, but the skills developed can be applied to serious topics in your life such as business practices or health decisions.

Flexibility will also be increased by reducing mental obstacles. The mind has a strong tendency to become attached to certain experiences, assumptions, views of one's self and the world, and ways of thinking and acting. Reducing attachments, in addition to increasing mental flexibility, also clears perception, reduces unwanted emotions, increases energy, and facilitates happiness and well-being.

With increased awareness and flexibility, you become more appropriately spontaneous; you more easily and naturally do what is called for by the situation. And all of this is associated with having greater freedom and choice.

## Breathwork

Although all of us have been breathing our whole lives, few were ever taught the basics of good breathing. As a result, most people some of the time, and some people a lot of the time, breathe incorrectly, which hurts the body's health and impairs the mind's functioning. This book teaches the basic principles of breathing and practices of breathwork that everyone should know, such as diaphragm breathing versus chest breathing and use of 4-2-4-2 controlled breathing.

Breathwork is also a major way of working with the universal life force, known in Chinese medicine as *chi* or *qi* (*ki* in Japanese). Chi, often pronounced "chee," is influenced by breathwork, mental training, and nutrition. Breathwork helps build up chi and transforms it into other forms of energy for the body. Some of the awareness practices will help direct chi into parts of the body that need it for healing and development. Working with this life force is a critical part of many healing systems around the world, including yoga; Ayurveda, the natural healing system of India; and many types of Native American shamanism and medicine.

Breathwork thus improves the health of the body, which helps the health of the mind. But there are two other reasons to include breathwork in a book focusing on mental training. First, breathwork is for most people the most effective way to relax the body, which then helps relax the mind. Relatedly, emotions and breathing are intertwined in complex ways; breathwork helps reduce unwanted emotions, which decreases stress and helps relaxation.

The second role of breathing in mental training is as an object of focus in early concentration practice and something to observe in early awareness training. The advantage here of breathing is that it is always available, very natural, and full of lessons.

## Resources

Specific references are listed in the "Resources" section near the end of the book. Information is drawn from well-established practices from around the world, including the following: Breathwork draws from Western respiratory science, Chinese medicine, and pranayama (the yogic science of breath). Flexibility draws from programs and practices to increase creativity and break mental habits. Procedures to reduce mental attachments come from Western, yogic, and Buddhist psychologies. And early training in concentration and awareness draws from the world's massive meditation literatures.

I have decades of experience practicing, teaching, and researching the procedures of this book. As a practitioner I have considerable experience applying the procedures to myself, and have fallen in many of the common traps. As a professor I have taught these procedures in college classes, professional workshops, and community programs. Feedback from all these groups, totalling literally thousands of people, has helped me determine what works best and how to present it. And in the course of my research, my students and I have done many studies on these practices, including self-control applications and effects in the brain.

## Not Religion or Philosophy

This is not a philosophy book to simply feed your thoughts—it is a manual of practices for mental development. There is nothing to believe or take on faith—you do the practices and see for yourself. This is not a book on religion—one can do the practices and learn to better use one's mind regardless of whether one is religious or not. But on the other hand, mental training can significantly improve religious or spiritual practices. For example, developing concentration helps Christian prayer and Hindu devotion, and developing awareness is basic to cultivating Buddhist insight.

Some of the practices in this book are adapted from the vast world literature on meditation. Meditation is not a religious practice; it is used for many different things, including healing the body, psychotherapy, and artistic creation. But meditation is also used as a spiritual practice in all the world's major religions, including Judaism, Christianity, Islam, Hinduism, Buddhism, and Taoism. The meditation-based practices in this book have no religious components, but if one wishes, they can later be applied to one's religious practices.

## Who?

The practices in this book can help almost everyone, regardless of age, schooling, gender, race, or profession. Of course, some people will be helped more than others, and there are great individual differences in terms of which practices are best for which people.

Parents and teachers can adapt the practices to better suit young people and/or the classroom. And others can adapt the practices for specific areas such as art, sports, and professions that require concentration and/or awareness (such as air traffic controller or emergency room nurse).

The practices in this book are very powerful and can significantly improve your life! But because they are so powerful, they are not right for everyone, at least at this time. For example, developing a quiet and aware mind is very good for most people, but for a very few individuals it can result in anxiety or problematic memories. So if any of these practices causes you to become agitated or upset, judge the degree of discomfort. If the discomfort is small, you can probably work through it and eliminate it with skills you learn in this manual, and thus improve your life. But if the practices cause great discomfort, perhaps you should stop doing them until you consult with a mental health professional familiar with mental training.

The breathwork practices will greatly help almost everyone, but they may need to be altered for people with breathing problems such as asthma. Similarly, sitting for an extended time might be part of some of the practices, and this could be harmful for some people with back problems. In cases like these, you may wish to consult your health advisor about how to modify the practices and do them within your limitations.

For example, people with asthma often breathe faster than others, resulting in them breathing out too much carbon dioxide and not enough oxygen getting to the cells. Breathwork for such people may involve diaphragm breathing (described in the next chapter), pausing before inhaling, and decreasing length of inhalation. A second example is people with back problems, who may decide to do some of the exercises lying down rather than sitting.

# Format

This manual is divided into five levels, each with its own skills, challenges, and discoveries; each level is a prerequisite for the next level. Thus, people work at their own rate, staying at one level until they are ready to move to the next level. However, there are great individual differences in mental training. For example, some people develop concentration faster than awareness, while for others it is the opposite. Or, some people need to spend more time on breathwork than flexibility, while the reverse is true for others. Thus, when using the manual, feel free to move through the different levels at different rates for each of the skills being developed. For example, at one time some of you might be at level I in concentration, level II in awareness, and level III in flexibility. This allows you to individualize the manual to suit yourself.

The image of the untrained mind being like a drunken monkey is a common metaphor in many Asian cultures. This monkey will be described in much more detail at level II. As you progress, you will learn many important things about your drunken monkey. And you will have many funny stories to tell.

There are two very important points regarding the use of the manual. The first is that you must *do* the practices, not just read about them. These are skills to be gradually cultivated, not just more stuff to think about. All the time spent developing these skills you will get back many times over. Think of it as an investment with very generous benefits. For example, you will become more efficient, such as students who need less study time as a result of developing concentration. And the mental training will reduce the biological diseases and psychological baggage that are sapping your time and energy.

The second important point in manual use is to take your time. Be patient and gentle with yourself, and do not advance to the next level until you are comfortable and ready. Do not rush your practices. You can certainly read ahead and sample practices from various levels, but the emphasis of your practice must be at the appropriate level. Moving too quickly through the levels is a very common mistake. In the long run, rushing will actually slow down your overall mental training and create some unnecessary problems. It is very important to master the basic skills of each level before moving on to the next level for that skill.

This manual is designed to help and guide you for many years; you won't have to get a follow-up manual. And you don't have to wait for years to get significant benefits—these will start coming right away. In addition, you will see and feel more and more benefits as your practice develops.

Now it is time to get started on this truly great adventure that will change your life. Remember, don't rush, do the practices, and most importantly, enjoy yourself and have fun on this journey.

# Level I

# Novice

The novice level is where everyone begins. There is no problem with being a novice; on the contrary, it is great you are beginning a journey that will significantly improve your life. It's not good to skip the novice level or move through it too quickly. It's important to start here and master the lessons of this level before moving on. Be honest with yourself, be patient, and have fun.

## Time and Place

Eventually, the mental training you will learn can be done almost anywhere and anytime. But at first, it is more effective to simplify the situation so you can devote all your attention to mental practice, minimizing distractions.

First is finding a time of day for the practices. Your schedule permitting, it is usually best to do the practices at about the same time each day, at least five days a week. It should be a natural part of your daily routine. If, instead, each day you wait to see when the practice will fit in, or when you are in the mood to do it, soon you won't be doing the practices at all. Find a good time and simply do it.

For some people, the morning is a good time to practice. Eventually you will be able to begin the day with a mind that is focused and clear and a heart that is open, which will be a great help in whatever you need to do each day. After getting up and going to the bathroom, you might do some type of exercise, such as walking or yoga. Relaxing during this time will help the mental practice.

For other people, early evening is a good practice time. It is a nice way to gradually relax and get free from the stresses of the day, and perhaps then be more fully present with others. After the work and chores of the day are largely over (and probably after the evening meal) is a good time.

Of course, you can practice any time of day that works for you, and more than once per day if possible and desirable. It is good to be relaxed but not too tired. Activities that help you relax such as listening to music, breathwork, or doing smooth stretching exercises help prepare you for mental practice. At first during mental practice you will have a tendency to fall asleep, so it is good if you are not too tired. Similarly, it is good to not be too full from a meal, as this may make you physically tired and/or mentally sluggish.

How long to practice each day will vary with what level you are at and the exercises you are doing that day. But you will be surprised that not much time is necessary for real accomplishments. At first, fifteen minutes a day will be good. During mental practice, your sense of time will often change; sometimes time will seem to go very slowly, sometimes very fast. If you need to be aware of when some time arrives, such as time to go to work or school or walk the dog, you can periodically glance at a clock. Better for most people is to set a timer that alerts you with a gentle tone or music.

Having established a time for practice, you now need a place. The practice area should be someplace where you won't be disturbed, such as the bedroom with the door closed. Make sure that people who live with you understand and respect this private time. Turn off all phones and perhaps put pets somewhere else. You can add props to your practice place; this is helpful to some people, but not necessary. For example, you might have a robe to wear or a special cushion to sit on that you only use during mental practice. You might burn some incense or play some music, as long as the music is simple background music which does not attract your attention or involve you.

At first, for most people, practicing inside is usually best; there are fewer things to deal with and fewer distractions. But if you wish, periodically practice outside. Nature can be very helpful in mental training. Try sitting in a garden, next to a tree, beside moving water, or at the shore of a lake or sea.

## Form

Form refers to what you do with your body during mental practice. Eventually form will be irrelevant; you can work with your mind almost no matter what your body is doing. But at first, particularly when training concentration and awareness, it is best to keep things simple: set the body down and focus on the mind.

For most people sitting is the best form. Sitting might be in a chair with feet flat on the floor or sitting on the floor on a cushion with legs crossed. In either case your back should be fairly straight up and you should not be leaning in any direction—forward, backward, or to either side. Hands should be placed in your lap, and your head should be tilted slightly down to the front.

Although it is not necessary, you might want to be more specific about the form. For some people this helps them be more focused and grounded in the body. For others it is a way to encourage being more precise in what one does. And for others it helps balance the flow of energy in the body. Here are some possible ways to be more specific with your form: Place your hands palm up on top of each other, so fingers are on top of fingers and the thumb tips touch each other. Keep your arms slightly away from the sides of your body. Be sure your head is not turned to the side. Your ears should be in line with your shoulders. Put the tip of your tongue gently on the roof of your mouth, which in Chinese medicine is understood to complete an energy circuit.

A second form for the body is lying down. This form is good as an occasional change from sitting, or for people who can't sit very long, perhaps due to back problems. Whether sitting or lying, at first there will be a tendency to fall asleep. This tendency is more true for lying, which is why sitting is usually better. When lying, lie on your back with your arms by your sides and legs uncrossed.

For most people, the best form at first includes closing the eyes, which greatly reduces distractions. As an occasional variation, or if you are anxious with your eyes closed, have your eyes slightly open, but not actually looking at anything.

## Breathwork I

You have the time, place, and form; now you are ready to begin the mental training. You start by observing your breathing, becoming more aware of exactly how you breathe. This observing will help you breathe more effectively and increase the health of your body. Later you will learn how to use your breathing to reduce stress and anxiety.

First, pay attention to your diaphragm, a muscular sheet between your chest cavity and your stomach cavity. When you breathe in, particularly with deep breaths, your diaphragm goes down, massaging the organs in your stomach cavity and pushing your stomach out. When you breathe out, your diaphragm rises and pushes air out of the bottom of your lungs.

Sitting or lying quietly, put your attention on the internal feelings of your diaphragm rising and falling. Try to be aware of the various sensations associated with this movement. Spend one or two training sessions just observing the movement of the diaphragm. If you have trouble with this, don't be concerned. Just notice the effects of the moving diaphragm, particularly your stomach going in and out. To emphasize this, you might, for a little while, pull your stomach in during exhalation, and then relax it for inhalation.

Next is observing the complete breath. When breathing in, it is usually best to breathe through the nose, as the nose cleans, warms, and humidifies the incoming air. Of course, sometimes, such as when one has a cold, nose breathing is difficult. Exhaling through the nose is not as important, and sometimes exhaling through the mouth is better, such as when doing deep breathing exercises.

A complete in-breath has four stages. First is inhaling, ideally through the nose. Second is the filling of the bottom of the lungs. During this time the diaphragm contracts and falls, the lower ribs slightly expand, and the stomach rises. Third, the middle of the lungs expand, and there is outward chest movement. And then fourth, the top of the lungs fill, and the upper chest and shoulders might rise somewhat. During a complete exhale, everything is done in reverse. The top of the lungs empty, then the middle of the lungs as the chest contracts, and then the bottom of the lungs as the diaphragm rises.

Spend a week of practice time just quietly observing your breathing, noticing ever more subtle aspects to it. Occasionally, follow the breath through all the stages listed in the previous paragraph. Other times, stay focused on just one of the stages for a while, such as the chest movement as the middle of the lungs fill or empty. Encourage your complete breath to be smooth throughout. Notice any obstructions, and relax or free them. Use this as a time to relax. Imagine that when you are breathing in, you are bringing in relaxation. You might say "calm and relaxed" to yourself as you inhale.

When doing breathwork at this level and future levels, you might occasionally get dizzy and/or light-headed. (For example, breathing too quickly can reduce oxygen to the body and cause dizziness, feelings of breathlessness, and lack of concentration.) If this happens, stop what you are doing, relax, and recover. Then alter the exercise, such as breathing less deeply or less frequently, until you find a way to continue and not get dizzy or light-headed. Also, if you have heart problems and notice that breathwork causes your heart to beat fast or irregularly, stop the breathwork until you consult with your heart specialist.

There are four common bad habits of breathing: mouth breathing, overbreathing, breath holding, and chest breathing. When observing your breathing, see if any of these apply to you. In mouth breathing one tends to breathe too much through the mouth. Periodically throughout the day check your breathing to see if you are mouth breathing, and/or have someone point out to you when you are mouth breathing. In overbreathing the amount of time to inhale is greater than the time to exhale. This is opposite to the way is usually should be, with more time to exhale than to inhale. To check this out, count or time your inhalations and exhalations. If you are overbreathing try to shorten your inhalations. Many people overbreathe when they are distressed. In breath holding there is not a smooth transition from inhalation to exhalation. Rather, the person catches and holds his breath, perhaps with some struggle to initiate the exhalation. This is particularly common during exercise. Look for this, and if it occurs, relax and smooth out the breathing. Sometimes relaxing the stomach after inhalation can help.

Particularly important is the difference between diaphragm breathing and chest breathing. Diaphragm breathing—also called deep breathing or yogic breathing— is the healthiest way to breathe. As described above, it involves the diaphragm to best empty and fill the lungs. Diaphragm breathing is very important, since 70 percent of the body's waste is expelled by the lungs! In chest breathing the diaphragm is not adequately used, rather it is the chest muscles that are doing most of the work. This is the type of breathing that one does when one is frightened or angry. It is good for emergencies, but not for overall breathing. Chest breathing does not work the lungs effectively and keeps the body stressed. Unfortunately, many people chest breathe far too much for the health of their body and mind. And most of these people are not aware of when they are chest breathing or when they switched from diaphragm breathing.

By learning to observe your breathing, as described above, and then periodically observing your breathing throughout the day, you will learn to notice when you are chest breathing and diaphragm breathing. Particularly observe your breathing when you are under pressure, stressed, or emotionally upset. Whenever you notice you are chest breathing, switch to diaphragm breathing. Stop what you are doing if possible, focus on your breathing, and take a few deep breaths. This practice may be one of the best things you can do for the overall health of your body, mind, and spirit.

To check your breathing, lie on your back, with knees bent and feet apart and flat on the floor. Put your palms flat against your lower rib cage with the middle fingers just touching. Inhale deeply and see if your fingertips are forced apart. With good deep breathing they will separate, perhaps by an inch or two. Then put one hand on your stomach and one on your chest. Breathe deeply and notice when the hands move and whether one moves more than the other.

## Moving On

There is much to be learned about your breathing at level I breathwork. Take your time and joyfully explore. Learn how to gradually improve your breathing, during practice times and throughout the day. Move on to level II breathwork when the following is true: You can easily observe all stages of complete breathing, including the nose, chest, and diaphragm or stomach. You can feel the difference between chest breathing and diaphragm breathing, and periodically intentionally shift from chest breathing to diaphragm breathing.

## Awareness I

As you progress through this book, you will gradually become more and more aware: more aware of your body, feelings, thoughts, and mental processes; and more aware of other people and the world around you. This awareness will bring you more health, happiness, choice, and freedom. But first, let us consider what awareness is.

Awareness refers to the conscious aspect of your mind. When your ears pick up a sound, you may be conscious of music or a voice. When your brain is planning how to respond to a situation, you may be conscious of a thought about your intentions. This awareness is very common and obvious. But what is not well-known is that you can learn how to be *more* aware. There are two related aspects to this—first is becoming aware of things you weren't aware of before. Second is your awareness becoming sharper and clearer. You perceive things more directly and accurately, with less distortion and confusion. You are sobering up the drunken monkey. In Buddhist psychology this type of awareness is called "mindfulness," and cultivation of mindfulness is the most important Buddhist practice.

Trickier is understanding what awareness is *not*. Awareness is not thinking, evaluating, or reacting; it is simply being aware. For example, the neighbor's dog starts barking when you are resting. Your mind identifies the sound and you have the thought "There's that dog again!" This thought is not awareness; it is just a thought. The thought may lead to another thought, such as "Why don't the neighbors keep that dog inside?" This reaction to the barking is not awareness; it is just a thought. Awareness is present to the extent that you are conscious of these thoughts, such as consciously noticing you are having thoughts about the barking dog. But all of this happens very quickly, and people are readily pulled into their thoughts, so the role of awareness is small. Later, as you become more aware, you will control your thoughts rather than them controlling you. But for now it is simply important to remember that thinking is not awareness, although you can be aware of thinking.

Similarly, you may emotionally react in some way to the dog's barking, such as getting mad. But any type of reaction is not awareness—awareness is being conscious of the reaction, such as noticing a change in breathing related to getting mad. The point is that awareness does not do anything; it simply notices what is happening. You notice the sights, sounds, and memories that come to you. You notice the feelings and thoughts that are brought forth. And you notice how you respond to these feelings and thoughts. Awareness is a passive observer, a neutral witness. It does not choose, think, or evaluate; it *observes* choosing, thinking, and evaluating.

These distinctions may be somewhat unclear or confusing at this time—don't be concerned! As you become more aware, all of this will become very clear and obvious to you. And this manual will guide you to become more aware. The first appendix in the back of the book is an Awareness Questionnaire, which will help you understand and evaluate your awareness. Answer this questionnaire now and periodically as you progress through this manual. By doing this, your understanding of awareness will become sharper and you will be able to see where you are progressing quickly and where slowly. For example, you may discover that you are becoming much more aware of your actions, but not as much of your feelings. This discovery may cause you to actively develop more awareness of feelings. For two reasons it is best not to write your answers to the questionnaire in this book. First, you will be taking the questionnaire many times. And second, you don't want your previous answers to influence your current answers. Write your answers on a separate piece of paper or photocopy the questionnaire. In either case, date your answers and see how they change over time. Although you will have a number score from most items on the questionnaire, don't combine these scores in any way. Rather, each time you retake the questionnaire, compare your answer for each item with your previous answer to the same item. Notice areas where your awareness is increasing and areas that need more attention. Notice when an item that was unclear before (marked X) now makes sense with your increased awareness.

## Exercise One

An excellent time to develop awareness is during breath-work like you have just learned to do. For now just sit or lie quietly and put your attention on your breathing. Don't be concerned about how you are breathing at this time; rather, put your emphasis on gradually being more and more aware of the fine aspects of breathing. Just let breathing go naturally and observe it in greater and greater detail. Put your attention on the breath at the tip of the nose. Notice how the air swirls around your nose and lip as you breathe in and out through your nose. Notice how the air you breathe in is cooler than the air you breathe out.

## Exercise Two

After watching your breathing at the tip of the nose, switch your attention to the rising and falling of the diaphragm and/or the stomach, as you did during breathwork. But now don't be concerned about how you are breathing, rather encourage yourself to gradually become more and more aware of feelings in this part of the body related to breathing. Minimize thinking here; just become more aware of your body.

## Exercise Three

Next switch your attention to following a whole cycle of breathing, as you did in breathwork. Feel the sensations in your body as the breath comes in through the nose, enters the throat, and goes into the lungs. Follow the breath back out as you exhale. Feel the sensations related to movement of your stomach, diaphragm, chest, and perhaps shoulders. Simply feel, don't think or evaluate. Notice positive feelings that accompany breathing, and notice any obstruction to breathing, or pain or stress. Don't be pleased or concerned about any of this at this time, just notice. When watching a complete cycle of breathing, notice there is a pause after inhaling before you begin exhaling, and a pause after exhaling before inhaling. Be aware of these pauses and any feelings associated with them.

For a while, perhaps a couple of weeks, have separate times for breathwork and awareness of breathwork. During breathwork, cultivate awareness but emphasize correct breathing. During awareness training, just let the breathing go naturally and emphasize passive awareness. These can be combined in the future, and you will develop awareness and work on your breathing at the same time.

## Body Scan

Another awareness practice is the body scan, a popular practice in yoga and in clinics for stress and pain. This is a simple practice that will help you become more aware of your body and relax and heal your body. The body scan can be done standing or sitting, but at first it is probably best done lying down. Very slowly let your awareness move through your body, beginning at the toes and moving to the head. Move your attention slowly and notice whatever you encounter. Don't try to force awareness, let it happen. One possible sequence through your body would be: right toes up to pelvis, left toes up to pelvis, pelvis to torso to shoulders, down right arm to fingers and back up, down left arm and back up, and then shoulders to neck to face to back of head to top of head. But you can devise a sequence that works best for you. Do a body scan at least once a day, five times a week, for a few weeks. After that, do it however often it is useful.

As an awareness practice, each time you do a body scan encourage yourself to become more aware of your body, noticing subtler and subtler details. Notice any stress or discomfort in your body. Notice if there is any numbness in some parts of the body. Notice if it is easier to be aware of some parts of your body than others. Is it easier to be aware of the front of your body than the back? Are you aware of your heartbeat? Can you be aware of the cavity of your torso, the space within your body. Do any parts of your body seem alien to you, somehow not truly part of your self?

## Moving On

Consider moving to level II awareness when the following are true: You understand what awareness is and how it differs from thinking and reacting. You have spent considerable time learning to become more aware of your breathing and body, and are now much more aware of these than you were when you began.

# Relaxing

Relaxing helps breathwork, awareness training, and concentration training, which is why it is helpful to relax before doing any of these. In turn, breathwork and awareness training will gradually help you to relax more. Switching from chest breathing to diaphragm breathing is a very powerful relaxation practice for some people. This practice involves learning to be aware of your breathing, so you notice when you are chest breathing and have the skills to switch to diaphragm breathing. Periodically when doing breathwork imagine that with each inhalation you are breathing in relaxation, and with each exhalation you are breathing out stress and anxiety. You might visualize these with shapes and/or colors, such as breathing in soothing white light and exhaling a dark mist of tension.

After doing body scans for a while as awareness training, you can modify the scans to also make them a good way to relax your body. When you notice tension in some part of your body, relax and let the tension flow out. For each part of your body that you attend to, imagine that you are actively breathing into that body part, with the breath bringing in relaxation. Then passively let the breath flow back out and bring tension with it. Let hardness dissolve into softness. In Chinese medicine it is understood that when you focus your awareness on some part of your body, as during a body scan, you are bringing life force (chi/qi) to this body part. This will help energize and heal this area. Thus, spend extra time with any part of your body that needs such help. Places that want healing may draw your attention to them. You might imagine that you are sending energy, healing, or love into that body part. Such imagining will actually have a physical effect.

## Muscle Relaxation

In Western psychology one of the most powerful forms of relaxation is muscle relaxation, also called deep muscle relaxation and progressive muscle relaxation. In this practice you gradually go through your body tensing and relaxing muscles. As a result of awareness training during this time you gradually learn to be more aware of tension and relaxation in your body. Then in real life situations when you start to get tense or anxious, you will notice it and relax, and eventually, your body will do this automatically. But that is later. First, it is necessary to begin awareness of muscle tension.

During body scans you are actively looking for tension to relax. To help this we now add to body scans tensing and relaxing muscles. A detailed description of muscles to be tensed and how to tense them is found in Appendix II. For example, say during your body scan that you are currently focused on your right hand. What you would add at this point is making a tight fist with your right hand and then gradually opening your fist and letting the tension flow out and letting your hand relax. During this time you want to be very aware of exactly what the tension feels like. Equally important, you want to be very aware of what it feels like when the tension changes to relaxation, and what relaxation feels like.

This muscle tensing practice should be done a number of times to improve awareness of the body. Some of you may choose to do it more, particularly if you have a need to relax and/or are aware of a lot of tension in your body. If you do continue, begin with the individual muscle groups listed in the appendix. This approach allows you to give specific attention to each muscle group, perhaps spending more time with muscles that your body scans suggest need additional work. After doing that many times, combine these groups so that you are tensing and relaxing groups of muscles, such as all the muscles in your right hand and arm. After a few rounds of that, see if you can relax the muscles without tensing them. Finally, throughout your day periodically notice any tension in your body and relax it.

Any type of relaxation practice can sometimes be improved by giving yourself relaxing suggestions. Make up your own or try a variation of one or more of the following: My breathing is slow and deep. Each breath relaxes me more and more. My legs (or other body part) are heavy and relaxed. My leg muscles are smooth and relaxed. Warmth is flowing into my legs. My whole body is relaxing more and more.

## Concentration I

Concentration is the ability to keep the mind focused on one thing; it is sometimes called one-pointedness. It involves getting the drunken monkey to stop running around so much and stay in one place. Here are some very common examples of lack of concentration: Jim is listening to music he enjoys, but much of the time he is not hearing the music, rather his mind is jumping to various thoughts about music, plans for the day, and concerns about his girlfriend. Stan needs a good night's sleep for an important day tomorrow, but instead of sleeping he is kept awake by a mind running through the next day's events. Rod is studying for an exam and has just read through a page of a text, but he has no idea what is on that page because his mind was jumping around. Kaitlin and Josh are disagreeing about how to deal with their son, but when Kaitlin is talking, Josh is not fully listening; rather he is reacting to what Kaitlin says and planning what he will say.

You will learn how to keep your mind focused, a skill that philosopher/psychologist William James considered the most important part of one's education. With this skill you will enjoy sensory pleasures much more, such as music, food, and sex. People who are trying to lose weight can eat less of some food, yet have more pleasure from the food than before learning to concentrate. Students learn how to stay focused on their lessons, and thus learn better in less time. People learn how to listen better to others, which improves their relationships. Athletes improve in their sports, such as being better able to keep their eyes on the ball or being less distracted by others. Artists learn how to get their selves out of the way and become immersed in the creative act. This is a small sample of the benefits you can enjoy as you develop concentration.

Concentration training will begin by keeping your attention on your breath. Later you can practice with other things, such as listening to music. Most people find this fairly challenging at first because they have such little control over their minds. As a result, many people give up early, convinced they can't learn to focus their minds. Don't be concerned if you find this difficult at first, you are just beginning to get control over your mind. Be patient and don't upset yourself! If you simply do the practices as described below, you will gradually develop concentration, even if at times it doesn't seem to you that you are making progress. You are. If you regularly do the practices, after a few weeks you will gradually start noticing the differences in your life, such as the beginning of some of the benefits listed above.

At the novice level the goal is to begin developing basic focus of the mind, one-pointedness. Later on you will discover that as the mind stays focused and does not jump around as much, the mind relaxes and becomes more tranquil and quiet. As the mind relaxes, it causes the body to relax. So if you choose, you eventually will possess the world's three most effective ways to relax body and mind: quieting the mind, muscle relaxation, and breathwork.

Still further along, as you learn more to quiet and focus your mind, you will gain control over your thoughts. Currently certain situations, memories, or thoughts can easily evoke unpleasant or problematic thoughts, which in turn can cause emotions such as anxiety, anger, jealousy, or worry. You probably can't do much about this, although maybe you can keep the emotions from getting out of hand. In the future, with advanced awareness and concentration skills, you will be able to get free from thoughts and stop or change those that are harmful. But all of this is for you to look forward to down the road. Let us get back to the here and now and start at the beginning of the road of concentration.

You'll be ready to begin concentration practice after you have spent a couple of weeks doing the breathwork and awareness of breath exercises discussed above. Begin by relaxing and then sitting or lying quietly observing your breathing. Next, put your attention on your breathing, either at the tip of your nose or the rising and falling of diaphragm or stomach. Breathe naturally and don't be concerned about how well you are breathing or how aware you are of the breathing; now it is time to emphasize concentration.

Mental labeling can be useful here. If you are focusing on the breath at the tip of the nose, very gently in the back of your mind say "in" when you breathe in and "out" when you breathe out. If you are focused on the rising and falling of the diaphragm or stomach, then gently say "rising" and "falling." Experiment with this labeling at different times. For some people it is helpful, for others it gets in the way.

Now, focus your mind on your breathing. It probably won't stay there very long. Soon it will run off to a sound, feeling, or thought. As soon as you are aware that your attention has left your breathing, gently and firmly bring your attention back to your breath. Again it won't stay long, and again you gently and firmly bring it back. That is all you need to do! Don't try to hold your attention on your breath, that won't work. Just keep bringing it back. Don't try to block other things from coming into your mind or grabbing your attention, that won't work. Just notice where your mind goes and gently bring it back to the breath. Sometimes this will be easy, sometimes hard. Some days you will feel you made progress, some days you will feel you did poorly. None of this matters! All that is important is that you do the practice regularly, regardless of how you evaluate your progress. Do this practice at least ten to fifteen minutes a day, at least five days a week. Do it longer whenever you wish. Again, be patient here! If during a ten-minute practice session your mind is focused for just one minute, you will benefit.

At the novice level, breathwork, concentration, and much of awareness is focused on breathing. Hence, there is a lot of overlap in these practices. At first it is important to keep these separate, at least for a few weeks. Then you can combine them into one practice. You sit or lie watching your breathing, cultivating awareness and adjusting your breathing as appropriate. You don't stay focused on one aspect of breathing, such as at the tip of your nose. Rather, your focus will move from one breathing area to another. But wherever your focus is, whenever your mind leaves the breath, you gently and firmly bring it back. Some days or some times within a practice session you may emphasize awareness over concentration, other times you may emphasize concentration. Experiment with different things. Be playful, and have fun.

## Moving On

Advance to level II of concentration when the following is true: You know the difference between when your mind is focused and when it is not. Even though your mind still jumps around during most practice sessions, you periodically have experienced short periods of time where your attention stayed on the breath. You have probably come to realize that you currently have less control over your mind than you previously thought you did. No problem, you are gaining control now.

# Attitude I

Attitude is the mental set with which one approaches situations. For example, some people have a positive attitude toward the world, seeing it as fun and challenging. Others have a negative attitude, seeing the world as unpleasant and problematic. Obviously the person with a positive attitude will have a happier and more effective life than the person with a negative attitude. As you will see, attitude is a very important part of mental training, a part which is often overlooked.

Attitude includes moods, associations, expectations, and intentions. Consider Steve's attitude toward the program of this book. His mood is positive and excited; this is something he has wanted to do for a while, and now he has an opportunity. He has done some reading on topics similar to this book and has done some yoga and meditation, so he has positive personal associations to some of the practices. Steve has strong positive expectations for his journey guided by this book, based on his beginning experiences at the novice level and his looking through the book to see where he is headed. And Steve intends to really give this project his best shot and to do all the exercises as described. Ralph, on the other hand, is not very optimistic about whether this book can help; he has tried stuff like this before and he believes it doesn't work for him. Ralph will skim through the book and sample a few exercises, but right now his life is filled with things that seem more important. So who will most profit from the book, Steve or Ralph?

The importance of attitude is often under appreciated. This is because almost everyone is very inaccurate about their own attitudes; people generally perceive their attitudes as being much more positive, supporting, loving, and so forth than they actually are. Throughout this book when recommendations are made relative to attitudes, don't overlook their importance by saying things such as "I already do that" or "That doesn't apply to me." Rather, really reflect on the suggestions related to attitude, and realize that whatever your current attitude, it can be improved in ways that will help you. There is a lot of subtlety here and much more can be learned than it first seems.

The two aspects of attitude that are stressed at the novice level and all levels are to act with intention and have fun. Act with intention means to take your time and actually do the exercises, not just read and think about them. This is not a philosophy book or inspirational reading, it is a manual, a workbook. What you learn will only come from doing the practices and seeing for yourself. Act with intention means to do it now, no excuses or procrastination. If not now, then when? Act with intention means to accept where you are right now and get started, not wish you were somewhere else or things were different.

Don't make a big deal of all of this, just do it. Don't make the exercises into unpleasant tasks, just do them. Don't make a big melodrama out of this journey, just get moving. For example, say you decide to floss your teeth at least once a day. Ideally, you would just simply do it regularly. You wouldn't struggle each day with the thought of the terrible task of flossing. And you wouldn't run around town bragging about how you are now a flosser. Ideally, you would just floss. You don't need to know the history of floss or build a temple to floss, just simply floss regularly. Similarly with the practices in this book, just do them. You can later evaluate them, modify them, emphasize the ones that are best for you, and read more about them. But first, just intentionally do the exercises!

The second part of the attitude is to have fun. Yes, these are serious practices, and yes, you can significantly improve your life. But relax into the journey and enjoy it. Don't make the exercises into serious or heavy tasks, just do them and enjoy what you encounter and learn. Approach the practices with playful curiosity, be an amused explorer of your own mind. Isn't your mind interesting? Doesn't it periodically amuse you? Be an investigator with a sense of humor. Try doing some of the practices with a slight smile on your face. What if you fall into some trap, repeat a mistake, or do something silly or stupid? What fun! Laugh it off, and keep moving.

## Moving On

Of course you don't move past the novice level until you have adequately done the exercises of this level. But you also must have developed a true commitment to continue the journey, a journey of skill building, not just thinking. You are prepared to continue doing the practices despite the obstacles life will present to you. Also, before moving to the next level, you need to have spent considerable time and reflection on how to have more fun with the practices and the journey. You might also reflect on how to have more fun in your life in general. Future levels will add to attitude, but acting with intention and having fun are basic and will always apply.

# Flexibility I

With the flexibility exercises you will learn to think better and more creatively. You will learn how to get out of mental ruts, think in new ways, and discover new ideas. You will learn how to problem-solve better, whether at work or home.

There are two aspects to increasing mental flexibility. One aspect focuses on creativity, discussed next in terms of lateral thinking. The second aspect is getting free from obstacles and attachments that limit and bind the mind. This aspect will be discussed shortly in terms of making mistakes and being wrong.

## Lateral Thinking

Edward de Bono is the creator of many practices, programs, and books designed to improve thinking. He deals with many different aspects of thinking, but mental flexibility is a major component. Relative to this he makes an important distinction between what he calls "vertical thinking" and "lateral thinking." One is not better than the other; you need both.

In vertical thinking you stay focused on the task and head in a clear direction, such as toward a solution to a problem. Thinking is logical and sequential, and you try to be correct at each step along the way; you stay inside the box of correctness. In vertical thinking you avoid and exclude irrelevant ideas and intrusions, and you follow the paths of thinking most likely to lead to the goal. To the extent that thinking is taught in the schools, it is usually vertical thinking.

Lateral thinking, on the other hand, has different goals—its purpose is to generate a number of new ideas. Hence, lateral thinking does not head toward a specific goal, rather it moves in various directions that elicit new thoughts, freely jumping around. Lateral thinking readily moves outside of the correctness box into areas that are clearly "wrong," such as ideas that are illogical, impractical, or irrelevant. Consideration of these "wrong" ideas may reveal a correct solution you were overlooking. So venturing outside the correctness box leads to ideas that bring you back into the correctness box at a different place than if you had always stayed within the box. Lateral thinking does not have to be correct at each step, can explore unlikely paths of thinking, and welcomes irrelevant ideas and intrusions that may stimulate new ideas.

Lateral thinking is a way to increase creativity and insight, and to escape from rigid mental patterns and ruts. Lateral thinking is a playful willingness to discover better ideas. Lateral thinking generates ideas, and then vertical thinking selects and develops some of the ideas.

The discussion so far has been pretty abstract, and perhaps a little hard to understand. So let us consider some concrete ways de Bono suggests will increase lateral thinking. One approach is to deliberately generate a number of alternative ways of looking at things, perhaps with a set quota. For example, if thinking about how to solve a parking problem, one might require oneself to come up with five very different ways to think about parking and related issues. Remember, it doesn't matter how logical or practical these ideas are. Another approach is to work backward, starting at the goal and moving back toward where we are currently. We might fantasize about the ideal parking solution and move backward toward where we are.

Brainstorming is a well-known practice for individual and group problem solving. Consider a group concerned with a parking problem. The group would generate ideas and pieces of ideas related to parking, with everything written down together for everyone to see. When generating ideas for this communal list, everyone playfully free-associates and spontaneously generates ideas, concepts, words, pictures, and diagrams. At this time the group is not evaluating any of these, and they may be silly, impractical, or wrong in some way. After idea generation has run its course, the group playfully reacts to different pieces and perhaps combines them in various ways. Hopefully all of this will stimulate new ideas that may help the problem-solving. Finally, vertical thinking is brought in to select and develop the ideas into an accepted solution.

De Bono also suggests the random stimulation method, a fun practice used by many advertising agencies. Here one takes a random concept, such as a word picked randomly from the dictionary, and adds it to the ideas being considered. De Bono gives the example of the random word "tadpole" being added to a discussion of teacher training. This word led to an image of teachers having tails, which led to the idea of training teacher assistants who would follow teachers around and help.

Other strategies for lateral thinking suggested by de Bono include questioning assumptions, breaking concepts into parts to be combined in new ways, use of analogies, and challenging categories and labels. As an exercise in lateral thinking, make up three more strategies for lateral thinking. Now if you wish, you might want to do the lateral thinking puzzles in the mental play section.

## Mistakes and Being Wrong

Related to lateral thinking is the second aspect of mental flexibility: the openness to making mistakes and being wrong. Making mistakes is a common part of many forms of learning, from kicking a ball to how to act on dates. It is often the best or fastest way to learn. However, many people consider mistakes a bad thing and try hard to avoid them, which then slows up their learning and impairs their creativity. In terms of lateral thinking, they try to stay inside the box of correctness. Some mistakes could be too costly and should be avoided. But too much avoiding mistakes can impair mental flexibility. Global thinker, inventor, and futurist Buckminster Fuller argued that contemporary leaders often suffer from the "mistake mystique," the belief that people should not make mistakes and the tendency to punish people for doing so. According to Fuller, mistakes are sins only when not admitted.

Related to making mistakes is being wrong. Everyone is periodically wrong; that's the nature of living. But for some people, being wrong is a problem, so they have trouble realizing when they are wrong and trouble admitting being wrong. Instead, they may generate reasons for why they weren't really wrong at all. This justification could happen with politicians, news commentators, academicians, doctors, scientists, fortune tellers, cult leaders, and many, many others.

Thus, mental flexibility is improved by being open to the fact that you will periodically be wrong, not being bothered by this fact, and being quick to admit when you are wrong. As you gradually develop in this aspect of flexibility, it will make your life more effective and happier. Relationships with others will improve, as when you freely admit you were wrong to a coworker, boss, lover, child, student, or someone else. It is very freeing.

That said, being wrong is not helpful if you don't learn from it. Also, there may be certain implications to having been wrong, such as something that needs to be fixed or an apology that must be given. But don't let such consequences keep you from realizing when you are wrong.

Many people define themselves in terms of their beliefs. Then, if one of these beliefs is wrong, it is hard to recognize and change because it is part of the sense of self. For example, Max held some unfavorable beliefs about how well women could perform in his workplace. He readily espoused these beliefs and they were part of who Max was as a person. In fact, these beliefs were wrong, got him in trouble with his female coworkers, and kept him from being promoted to a managerial position. Max was wrong and these beliefs were hurting him, but he could not let them go; they were part of who he thought he was. How much better Max's life would have been if he could have realized and admitted he was wrong and changed his attitude. What happened to Max is very common, something many people experience.

Thus, the first step is changing your attitude about making mistakes and being wrong. Rather than seeing them as being problems, recognize them as opportunities to learn, change, and grow. And have fun with all of this! As a practice, be on the alert for times when you are wrong, even if it is something very simple, such as what channel a TV show is on or the color of a car. Take delight in discovering when you are wrong! This practice will slowly train your mind to eventually notice much more important examples.

In addition to looking for when you are wrong, seek opportunities to admit being wrong. At first these may be simple situations, but with practice you will become more at ease and natural doing this.

De Bono suggests a thinking tool he calls PMI, which stands for "Plus, Minus, Interesting." When considering some choice or decision, first list all the plus or good points. Then list the minus or bad points, and finally list related interesting points. People often do something like this when deciding between choices. But in addition, PMI encourages seeing alternatives, rather than just looking for reasons to support one's current idea or perception. PMI helps with mental flexibility as it facilitates considering new and different ideas.

## Moving On

Before moving to the next level of flexibility, the following should be true: You understand the nature of lateral thinking, and you periodically utilize lateral thinking type of strategies. You have systematically applied lateral thinking to several topics of personal significance. You are free of the mistake mystique and readily notice and admit being wrong. And you have identified at least one major area where you were wrong and did something to make corrections.

# Mental Play

The mental play sections at each level contain playful ways of using your mind, such as logic puzzles. All the mental play exercises are optional; they are not necessary to the overall program of this book. If you enjoy some of the mental play exercises, do them and enjoy. If you don't enjoy them, feel free to skip them, but at least try a few. When doing any of these exercises, observe your thought processes and remember the attitude of having fun. You will also have some opportunities to experience being wrong.

The exercises will vary from quite easy to very difficult. Don't give up too early on the hard ones; you will enjoy the sense of satisfaction if you stay with them and figure them out, and you will learn more about your thinking. Almost none of the mental play exercises are original with this book; they are drawn from many sources. Some are fairly well-known, and a few are classics. The first three questions are warm-up puzzles to get your mind going. Questions 4–13 require mental flexibility, such as lateral thinking, for their solutions. For most of these questions there may be more than one right answer. Questions 14–17 are logic puzzles with one right answer. Answers for questions 5–17 can be found in Appendix III.

1. Should there be a law against a man marrying his widow's sister?

2. Why does a mirror reverse left and right, but not up and down?

3. If humans' knees bent the other way, what would a chair look like?

4. De Bono asks you to use specific lateral thinking strategies discussed earlier to come up with designs for the four following objects: an apple-picking machine, a cart to go over rough ground, a better umbrella, and an improved human body.

5. How can you stand behind a friend while this friend is standing behind you?

6. How can you stand on the same piece of newspaper as your friend without being able to touch each other?

7. Why are manhole covers circular instead of square?

8. Why do people who sell sardines pack as many of them into the can as possible?

9. How can you make a tennis ball go a short distance, come to a complete stop, and then go in the opposite direction? You may not attach anything to the ball, bounce the ball, or roll and spin it.

10. Cash prize in an automobile race goes to the driver whose car comes in last. But this might result in the drivers going slower and slower and the race never ending. How can you resolve this?

11. You are completely dealing out a full deck of 52 cards into four hands, as in bridge. In the middle of dealing you get interrupted and leave and come back. But when you return, you have forgotten where you were in the dealing. Without counting any cards, or getting any information from anyone, how can you continue dealing so everyone gets the same cards as if you had not been interrupted?

12. In a lightproof closet is a single light bulb. The light is off and the closet door is closed. There is no way to see into the closet. Down the hall are three light switches, all in the off position, one turns on the light in the closet, and the other two do nothing. You may flip the switches as you wish, but once you open the closet door, you may not touch the switches again. How do you determine which switch turns on the closet light?

13. You have two jars of pills, marked A and B, where all pills look, weigh, feel, smell, and taste identical. The number of pills in the two jars is unequal and unknown. Each day you must take exactly one A pill and one B pill. One day when pouring pills into your hand, by mistake you get one A and two B's. The three get mixed up. You could throw them out and start again, but do you have a better solution that doesn't waste pills?

14. A notebook costs a dollar more than a pencil. Together they cost $1.10. How much did each cost?

15. There are 10 black socks and 16 blue socks randomly mixed in a drawer. It is too dark in the room to tell blue from black. How many socks do you have to take out of the drawer before you can be sure you have a pair of the same color?

16. On an island are two classes of people: knaves who always lie and knights who always tell the truth. You meet three of them together (A, B, C). When you asked A if he is a knight or a knave, you cannot understand his answer. B then says "A said that he is a knave." To which C replies, "Don't believe B, he is lying." What are B and C?

17. You have a glass of water and a glass with an equal amount of wine. You now take a tablespoon of the water and mix it in the wine. Then you take a tablespoon of this mixture and put it in the water. Is there now more wine in the water glass or water in the wine glass?

# Level II

# STUDENT

If you have done the practices at level I and are now ready to move to the next level, congratulations! Your dedication will continue to pay off as you advance. You've stuck with it and had the wisdom and/or motivation to really grab hold of your life and start to do something significant. Wonderful! You now have the prerequisites to become a true "student" in the school of the mind. You have the basics in five general areas (concentration, awareness, breathwork, flexibility, and attitude) and now it is time to further hone these skills and build on them. As was mentioned before, you might progress through these five areas at different rates. For example, at one time a person might be at level I in concentration, level II in flexibility, and level III in breathwork.

You don't have to be at the same level in all five areas, and you move through each area at your own rate.

In level I you learned about time, place, and form; you were also given some suggestions about how often and how long. By now you have worked out what works best for you, and the expression "your way of practice" will refer to this. Of course, you will be continually modifying your way of practice as you learn more and as you adapt the practice to different situations. Also, although not many more recommendations will be made relative to how often and how long, you know the importance of doing the practices regularly for a moderate amount of time.

At the student level you will further develop your skills in the five areas. You will also get to know the drunken monkey, an interesting and troublesome character. As your journey continues, you will collect many stories about your exploits with this monkey.

## Drunken Monkey

In Buddhist psychology and the yogic sciences, the mind is often described as a wild or drunken monkey, sometimes jumping from limb to limb in a tree. In a common metaphor, the monkey lives in a room with six windows. The windows correspond to the five physical senses (seeing, hearing, feeling, smelling, tasting) and the mental sense (thinking, remembering, fantasizing, etc.). The drunken monkey, out of control, runs from window to window.

Once you wake up in the morning, the monkey starts running, sometimes slow and sometimes fast, darting from window to window. You might be able to entice the monkey to a specific window with something to see or taste, but it won't stay long. Most people have little or no control over their monkey minds. We don't want to hurt this monkey, but it must be tamed. The monkey can be a good servant, but it is a bad master. For people who have not trained their minds, the drunken monkeys are the masters. At the novice level you started to tame the monkey, and now you are ready to do more systematic taming.

Since you have your own personal drunken monkey, you may conceptualize your monkey however you wish. You choose the monkey's appearance, size, and sex. You can even name the monkey if you like. In all your dealings with the monkey, always remember the principle of having fun. The monkey does not want to be tamed and will try to talk you out of it or distract you into something else. Since the monkey is your mind, it (you) will come up with the best reasons and distractions that work against you.

Do not underestimate the monkey—it usually wins. Here are some typical things the monkey might get a person to think in order to stop the practices: "I've tried some of this before, and it doesn't work for me." "I can't do this because I am too young, too old, too smart, too busy (etc)." "I definitely want to do this, but now is not the time because..." "These practices are wasting time, when I have more important things to do." "My mind is working fine, now, don't mess it up." "These practices conflict with my beliefs about…"

As a student, you have to be on the alert for these types of monkey tricks. Don't let the monkey talk you out of doing the practices, regardless of how clever and convincing the arguments. If you think clearly about the monkey's arguments, you can usually see what is wrong about them. As practice, think about how you would refute the arguments in the previous paragraph and what you think your monkey will come up with.

Always remember the following: Learning to use your mind more effectively is one of the most important things you can do with your life; it will improve almost everything you do, and thus increase your happiness and health. To do this, you as a student must spend time developing skills— reading, thinking, and wishing will not work. Whatever time you spend developing these skills you will get back many times over for many reasons, including being more effective and efficient, and avoiding common traps. None of this has to have anything to do with religion and philosophy, but if you are religious or spiritual, these practices will help you on the path of your choice.

## Concentration II

At this level the best way of taming the monkey is through developing concentration. You try to keep the monkey at one object, such as your breath, or at one window, such as hearing. You continue the same basic practice that you already know: you put your attention on something, such as your breathing at the tip of the nose, and every time the monkey runs off, you gently and firmly bring your attention back to your breathing. The main practice is further development of concentration, as you have already begun at the last level. As your concentration improves, you will gradually tame the monkey; it will run around less frantically and slowly sober up. Be patient—sometimes you will make good progress taming the monkey, often it will run wild outside of your control.

Since the monkey does not want to be tamed, it has many tricks to distract you from developing concentration. For the examples it will be assumed that your way of practice is with your attention on the breath. Sometimes during your practice you may feel that there are spider webs on your body, that your body is getting heavier, or that you are starting to have an out-of-body experience. These are all monkey tricks; briefly notice them and return to your breath. Maybe you will have visual images or see lights of various colors. Again, just notice them and return to your breath.

Maybe during your practice you will have an insight about yourself or reality, or perhaps a solution to a problem will arise. Perhaps you will feel the necessity to stop the practice so you can think about what you have discovered, or maybe you feel you need to write it down so you won't forget. These are all monkey tricks. Whenever an insight or thought arises, just briefly notice it and return to your breath. If it is really important, you will remember it later and can think about it then. The practices of this book will lead to profound insights, but don't get distracted by less important insights the monkey tries to dazzle you with.

The monkey may tell you that your practice is not going well one day and it would be best to quit—don't fall for this. It is important to stay with the practice, regardless of how well the monkey says it is going.

For the duration of your concentration practice at the student level is one simple principle: No matter what arises, treat it as a monkey trick and return to your breath. This includes all feelings, images, thoughts, and memories.

In rare cases the monkey trick may cause anxiety or depression. If it is mild, and you can just notice and return to your breath, great. However, if the feelings are strong and keep occurring, you have two choices: First, you can stop the practices until you consult with a professional counselor familiar with these practices. Second, you can stay with the strong feelings, carefully observing them, until they lose their power and there is nothing more to learn from them.

In addition to monkey tricks, there are other distractions to concentration. Pain and itches are very common. If one of these arises, try just noticing it and returning to your breath. But if it persists and keeps pulling your attention to it, simply deal with it. Scratch the itch, massage the pained area, change your sitting position, or whatever. But while you are doing this, keep your focus on the related feelings in your body, such as the feelings related to re-crossing your legs or scratching your arm. Then return to your breath.

Another common distraction is an external sound that, for whatever reason, keeps pulling your attention to it. The distraction might be traffic, someone working nearby, or the sound of an air conditioner. You have tried just noticing the sound and staying with your breath, but you keep getting pulled back. When this happens, one solution is to make the external sound the focus of your attention. Stay with the sound; when your mind goes somewhere else, gently and firmly bring your attention back to the sound. Do this for awhile until the sound no longer has such a pull on your attention. Then return to your breath.

## Other Objects of Focus

So far breath has been the main focus during concentration. This is good and should be continued, but now it is time to add some additional objects of focus. Music is a good object for some people. Put your focus on listening to the music. Then, whenever your mind leaves the music, including to thoughts about the music, gently and firmly bring your attention back to hearing. For some people the feelings in different parts of their bodies during exercise are good objects. When doing some type of exercise, such as stretching, running, or working with weights, you would keep your attention on some part of the body, periodically changing the part you focus on.

What you need to do as a student is add at least two or three new objects of concentration to your practice. In addition to music and body, other possible objects are watching videos and movies, playing a video game or musical instrument, fishing, and making something. Pick something of importance and/or pleasure to you; it doesn't have to be one of the above examples. The primary goal for level II concentration is the further development of one-pointed concentration despite distractions, and using the breath and other objects of focus.

## Moment-to-Moment Concentration

So far, concentration has primarily been maintaining one-pointedness on a particular object, such as the breath at the tip of the nose. But in addition, there is also a more subtle and more applicable from of concentration known as moment-to-moment concentration (MTMC). After you are well into level II concentration, you can begin learning about and developing MTMC. The essence of MTMC is that even though your mind is moving from one object to another, you can still have precise one-pointed focus on whatever the mind is attending to. A practice to develop MTMC is very similar to your way of developing concentration on the breath. The difference is that you do not pick an object of focus and do not keep bringing your attention back to one object. Rather, you let your mind go where it will; you let go and don't choose. But wherever your mind goes, you try to bring to that object concentrated focus. Of course, this is much easier the less the mind is jumping around. MTMC is quite subtle at first, so don't be concerned if you do not totally understand it yet. You will in time.

## Moving On

You are ready to move to Concentration III when the following are true: You understand the tricks the monkey uses on you, and although it still periodically catches you, you don't stay caught long. Distractions to your concentration periodically arise, but most of the time they are short lived and not troublesome. You have a clear sense of how to concentrate your mind, and can usually easily do it, when you are aware and motivated. There have been many times in which you have maintained strong concentration on some object. And you have developed concentration using your breath as well as other objects.

# Awareness II

At the novice level the major object of awareness was the body, including breathing and muscle tension. Awareness of your body should always be part of your practice. From now on you should periodically intentionally focus your awareness on some part of your body, such as during exercise and breathwork. You might do it when you are relaxing or having something done to your body, such as massage or caressing. Putting your awareness on your body is often a good way to become more grounded, as when you are too lost in thoughts or are feeling spacey. You might focus on your breathing as a way to concentrate your mind and pull yourself back into awareness.

Becoming more aware of your body will help you notice when stress or anxiety is building up. This awareness will make it easier for you to stop or reduce the stress or anxiety. For example, you might notice tension building up in your neck and shoulders. If you notice it early enough, you can do something about it before you develop a tension headache. Other body signals that might be stress-related include a wrinkled forehead, clenched teeth, tight chest, and lower back pain. Becoming more aware of your posture may result in your holding and moving your body in ways that produce less stress and strain. Poor posture, such as hunched-over shoulders, can impair optimal breathing.

Feelings in the body often precede actions and thoughts. By noticing the feelings, you may be able to stop an unwanted behavior. For example, your body may suddenly have some type of craving, as for food, drink, cigarette, alcohol, or another drug. Next, before you realize it, you are already eating a piece of candy or lighting up a cigarette. Then, the drunken monkey, who thrives during lack of awareness, comes up with various thoughts to explain or justify what you are doing. As you become more aware of the feelings of craving in your body, you will have more choice and self-control. Sometimes you will eat the candy, sometimes you won't; *you* have the choice, not the monkey. Learn to be more aware of your body's cravings.

Similarly, your body may also respond to situations with aversion, which leads to behaviors to reduce or escape from something. If you accidentally put your hand on something very painful, such as a hot burner on the stove, your body will immediately withdraw the hand. This action will not require the brain and will happen before you realize what is going on. The withdrawing of the hand is a simple reflex that only involves the spinal cord. To wait on the brain would be too slow. And to wait for the self to arise and withdraw the hand through an act of will would be disastrous. So the body simply and quickly withdraws the hand. Later, the brain will perceive the event and experience the pain.

But in other aversive situations you could have a choice. For example, as discussed above, when an itch arises during your concentration practice, you could just unconsciously scratch the itch. Or you could notice the itch and choose to scratch or not. If you unconsciously escape from a person or place when you feel aversion, the situation or person will probably continue to be aversive. But if you are aware of the aversion, then sometimes you may choose to not escape and let the aversion decrease. Becoming more aware of cravings and aversions is a critical part of being a student and making your life more effective and happy. The issue here is not what you do in the presence of a craving or aversion; rather, it is a matter of being aware and having a choice.

Perceptions and thoughts often cause feelings in your body. As you notice this more and more, you will better understand the interplay between your mind and body. You might notice that certain thoughts create stress or anxiety in your body, and therefore choose to reduce this type of thinking. Sometimes when you have an important insight, you might notice a sudden shift in body feelings and/or a sense of physical relaxation. This body sensation might help you recognize the importance of the insight.

## Basic Practice

The major formal awareness practice at the student level is a variation of the concentration practice you have already done. Consider your way of concentration practice. In this practice you notice where your mind goes, as to a sound or itch, and then bring your attention back to the breath, or whatever you are concentrating on. The "noticing" in this is the awareness component, which was secondary to the concentration component. Now the emphasis will be put on awareness, and concentration will be secondary.

During your way of practice, intentionally try to clearly notice wherever your mind goes. Say your practice is sitting quietly with your attention on your breathing at the tip of your nose. Attention is on your breath but then jumps to a sound and from there to a thought about the sound. Try to clearly be aware of the sound and then clearly be aware of the thought. If the sound or thought elicits craving or aversion, simply notice this emotional response and exactly how it feels. Eventually bring your attention back to the breath, which for now is of minor concern. Instead, try to see clearly whatever arises in your mind, including feelings, perceptions, and thoughts. Remember that you simply want to be aware, not necessarily react to what you are aware of. Awareness is different from and does not require thinking, judging, or emotional responding.

The above practice is hard to do if the monkey is too wild. Therefore, you need to have developed some degree of ability to concentrate and quiet your mind before beginning this awareness practice. And each time you do the awareness practice, it is usually best to first spend some time relaxing and quieting the mind. Then you can just let your mind go and see clearly where it goes. Whenever there seems to be a break between objects of awareness, you bring your attention back to the breath.

## Using Labels

Periodically during awareness training, experiment with the use of labels. When something visual arises in your mind, gently say "seeing" in the back of your mind. Use this label if the vision is caused by something you see through your eyes or is coming from your mind. For sounds, wherever they come from, gently say "hearing" in the back of your mind. For any feelings that come from your body, say "feeling." And for any type of thoughts, say "thinking." Occasionally you might use the labels "smelling" or "tasting." This labeling will force you to be more accurate about what you are noticing and sometimes it helps quiet the monkey by giving him something to do. Sometimes it won't be obvious which label applies; this may be due to not having a clear awareness and/or what you are aware of seems to require a combination of labels. After doing this basic labeling for a while, you may want to add some labels that cover common things you encounter, such as "planning," "intending," or "worrying."

## Combining Practices

After you become fairly skillful with the awareness practice, you can combine concentration and awareness training. During your way of practice you train both of them. Some days or sometimes within a daily practice you emphasize concentration, other times you emphasize awareness; you always cultivate both. You will learn to recognize what needs to be emphasized at any time. An important thing is to learn to be more aware of how concentrated your mind is, both during formal practice and throughout the day. More subtle, but equally important is learning to be more aware of how aware you are at any time.

## Moving On

You are ready to move to Awareness III when the following are true: You have become more aware of your body in a variety of ways and regularly, consciously attend to some parts of your body. You have learned how to cultivate awareness during your way of practice, and you know the difference between awareness and concentration. You can easily be aware of how concentrated your mind is, and you are becoming more aware of how aware you are at any time.

# Attitude II

At the novice level you learned the first two parts of the optimal attitude: act with intention and have fun! These continue to be very important. Now we will add parts three and four: make friends with yourself, and be in the here and now.

## *Make Friends with Yourself*

Say you have a good long-time friend named Roger. There are many things about Roger that bring you pleasure, a couple of things that periodically irritate you, and some ways you wish Roger would change for his own sake. As a friend, you encourage Roger to change in ways that are possible, and you learn to accept things that aren't going to change. But regardless of all of this, Roger is your good friend, whom you ideally love unconditionally. That is, you love Roger regardless of all of his strengths and weaknesses. He is your friend. But do you treat yourself the same way? Are you a good friend with yourself?

Most people are much harsher and less forgiving with themselves than they are with their friends. So you could probably profit from learning to be a better friend with yourself, particularly since you will be spending a lot of time with yourself. There are things you do which please you, things you do which upset you, and there are ways you wish or need to change. Fine, that is the way life is. Love yourself unconditionally regardless of all of this. This acceptance does not mean being blind to your mistakes or not encouraging yourself to learn, grow, and change. That is not how a good friend acts. You want to be open to being wrong and making mistakes (Flexibility I), but not upset yourself about this. And you want to encourage yourself to do things to improve your life, such as the program in this book. As a friend of yourself, you are pleased when you are actively doing something to make your life better (act with intention), and concerned when the monkey talks you out of it. Periodically when doing the practices in this book, you will not be a good friend to yourself. You will get irritated, frustrated, impatient, opinionated, and many other such negative reactions toward and about yourself. When one of these occurs, see it for what it is and make up with yourself. Unconditionally accept yourself, even when you are recognizing areas for improvement. If you say you can't accept yourself unconditionally, then accept yourself as someone who can't accept her or his self unconditionally. Regardless of where you are on your journey, accept yourself as you actually are here and now, and continue the journey with your friend.

## Here and Now

If you observe your mind for a while, you will discover that most of the time you are living in the past or the future;

you are rarely in the here and now. Part of the time you are caught up in memories of the past, recycling pleasant and unpleasant events. Part of the time you are lost in an imaginary future, filled with anticipations, plans, and concerns. Very rarely are you fully in the present. It often takes something dramatic, such as pain or a beautiful sunset, to momentarily pull you into the here and now. There is nothing wrong with having memories or making plans for the future. The problem is that most people spend way too much time lost in these mental places, and thus miss much of the beauty and pleasure happening in the here and now. So how do you be more in the here and now?

The key to bringing yourself into the here and now is concentration, with help from awareness. When you are aware that you are lost in the past or future, you concentrate on something in the present to bring you back to the here and now. This practice is often a good way to reduce the anxiety or boredom associated with the mental place you were lost in. The attitude component is the recognition of the importance and value of being in the here and now and doing something about it.

Say you are going to the park to meet your friend Roger for some activity, such as playing tennis or a picnic. The journey to the park is just time filler until you are there and the fun begins. So you consider the journey as just wasted time lost from your life, perhaps filled with daydreaming or music. Being in the here and now involves valuing the journey itself, not just seeing it as a means to an end. Anytime in the here and now is valuable! What are some examples from your life?

To better understand this, consider singing and dancing. The purpose of singing is not to get to the end of the song. The purpose of dancing is not to get across the dance floor. Singing and dancing are activities to be enjoyed and valued in themselves, not as means to some goal. The same is true with the practices in this manual. You choose to do the practices for the benefits they will bring you. But while doing the practices, you should not be in the past or the future—you should be fully in the here and now enjoying and valuing the practices themselves. Act with intention, leave the past and future alone, and have a good time in the here and now. One of the most profound understandings about personal and spiritual growth is that it is not so much a matter of getting there then, it is more a matter of being here now.

At the student level the emphasis of the four components of attitude is how they apply to the general practices of the program. As you come to understand them in this context, you will gradually realize how they apply to many different aspects of your life. For example, having fun is very important when dealing with the drunken monkey. But learning how to have more fun in life in general is important for many people. Look for more ways to have fun and not "maturing" into a person who forgets how to play. It includes being able to laugh at one's self and not letting the seriousness of one's personal melodrama become over-whelming.

As a student, it is very important that you regularly reflect on the four components of attitude: act with intention, have fun, make friends with yourself, and be in the here and now. At first do this reflection at least once a week, then once a month, and then periodically. At first reflect on how these apply to the practices in this book, and later how they also apply to your life in general. Such reflection is very important, as you will discover if you seriously and thoughtfully pursue it. Do this with a welcoming openness to discover and to learn.

Attitude is important and affects us all in very powerful ways. Make sure to give it the attention and reflection it requires. You may believe you do many of these things already, but you may actually be missing some important steps. As a student, you must realize there is much more to these four attitude components than you currently realize or understand. As a student you will actively reflect on how these relate to you and will cultivate awareness of them. You will know you are making progress if you are continually discovering new ways they apply to your life and finding more and more depth and subtlety to your understanding.

## Breathwork II

At the novice level you learned a lot about your breathing, from the breathwork exercises and awareness training. You have observed the full course of your breathing from nose to diaphragm, and you have learned how to alter and improve your breathing. Now, at this level you will learn how to further refine and alter your breathing by changing the rate of inhalation and exhalation. You will also learn additional ways to use breathing to reduce stress and anxiety. But first consider how to breathe during stretching exercises.

## Breathing During Stretching

Some type of stretching or hatha yoga should be an important part of most people's overall maintenance of the body, in addition to aerobic exercise and muscle toning. And this need for flexibility exercises generally increases with age. When doing stretching and bending exercises, it is important to pay attention to your breathing. First, try to breathe evenly and deeply without jerks and pauses, letting the body movements flow evenly and gently with the breath. Pay attention to when you are inhaling and exhaling. Generally speaking, you want to exhale when you are contracting, bending forward, compressing your stomach, or twisting. You want to inhale when are expanding, bending backward, opening your chest, or coming out of a stretch. Reflect on these general principles and think about how they apply to other exercises and activities you do.

## Breathing Rate

Observe how long it takes you to inhale versus how long to exhale. You can formally time this or simply count. You don't need exact measurements here, just an awareness of which takes longer. As a general rule, it is usually healthier for the exhalation to be longer than the inhalation. Breathing rate is something you should periodically check.

When you want to relax more, lengthen the time of exhalation and briefly hold your breath after exhaling. If you are feeling anxious, gradually lengthen the time of exhalation. If you need more energy, lengthen the time of inhalation and briefly hold your breath after inhaling. In all of this you need to experiment and find what works best for you.

Some cases of fatigue are helped by first lengthening exhalations for about a dozen breaths and then gradually lengthening inhalations. And some cases of depression are helped by having the same length of both inhalation and exhalation, and then gradually lengthening both.

The above ways of altering breathing rate to affect emotions and energy are drawn from Asian health systems, particularly pranayama (yogic breathwork) and Ayurveda (the natural healing system of India). The practices have been well established over thousands of years. Exactly how all this works biologically is very complex and yet to be fully understood. Here is some of what is known: The primary function of the respiratory system is to bring oxygen in and expel carbon dioxide. Part of this process includes maintaining the right acid/alkaline balance in the blood, optimal health requires the blood to be slightly alkaline. With excitement, stress, and activity carbon dioxide and other acids are produced, which results in automatic increases in breathing to bring in more oxygen and expel the excess carbon dioxide, and thus reduce the acidity of the blood. It is also well known that hyperventilation, quick shallow breathing, results in not enough oxygen getting to the body, which then triggers anxiety and irritability. Voluntary slowing of breathing rates thus reduces biological and psychological arousal. Also, there are lung diseases that affect breathing. Many of these can be diagnosed with pulmonary function testing, which measures the lungs' capacity to hold air, move air in and out, and exchange carbon dioxide and oxygen.

## Moving On

Before progressing to Breathwork III, the following should be true: You periodically monitor your breathing in various situations and alter it as needed. You have added to your overall awareness of your complete breathing the periodic awareness of the relative lengths of inhalation and exhalation. You have learned how to alter these lengths for the purpose of relaxation or energy. You are a true student of breathing.

# Relaxing

At the previous level you learned to relax using diaphragm breathing, body scans, muscle relaxation, and relaxing suggestions. Now we add a form of controlled breathing and the use of imagined scenes.

## Controlled Breathing

A simple but effective way to relax is 4-2-4-2 controlled breathing. Here you gradually inhale for a count of four, hold your breath for a count of two, gradually exhale for a count of four, hold your breath for a count of two, and then begin again. Spend some time experimenting with this until you find the speed of counting that works best for you. A nice variation is to eventually substitute the words "calm and relaxed" for the counts of two.

You now have two good ways to use breathing to relax: 4-2-4-2 breathing and deep/diaphragm breathing. Use whichever works best for you, or combine them. For example, you might first take a few deep breaths and then switch to 4-2-4-2 breathing. Whatever way to relax works for you, the next step is to look for opportunities to apply this practice during your daily life. Notice when you are starting to feel anxious or stressed. Perhaps you notice a change in your breathing, a build-up of muscle tension, an increased heart rate, or the monkey becoming more wild. When this happens, take a time-out from what you are doing, put your attention on your breath, and use your relaxing breathing practice. It might not be practical to do this immediately, but do it as soon as you can. Maybe you will need to do something first, such as get up from your desk, take off your sweater, go into another room, or step out the back door.

## *Imagined Scenes*

Practicing with imagined scenes is a good way to develop your relaxation skills and to reduce negative feelings you associate with particular people or places. Make a list of people, animals, things, places, and situations that cause unwanted negative feelings, such as stress, anxiety, fear, anger, or jealousy. For now, don't include very strong items that elicit intense feelings; you may want to do that later. Put the items from your list in a rank order with the top of the list the item that causes the most bad feelings down to the bottom of the list with the item that causes the least. Then close your eyes and relax, using your relaxing breathing practices and/or muscle relaxation. While relaxing, imagine something pleasant. While imagining, try to really put yourself in the situation and live it, as opposed to passively seeing something on a movie screen in your head.

After relaxing with your pleasant scene, switch to realistically imagining the least negative item on your list. Notice any feelings in your body that relate to becoming less relaxed. When you notice this, stop imagining the unpleasant item and switch to your pleasant scene. Do this back and forth between scenes until you can stay relaxed while imaging the bottom item. Then move to the next time, and slowly work your way up the list. This should be spread over many days, doing it about fifteen to thirty minutes a day, two or three times a week.

The above practice with imagined scenes is great awareness training to learn how to notice when you are becoming less relaxed and perhaps anxious, angry, or something else. As you learn to notice this earlier and earlier, you will have more and more self-control over these feelings and emotions. Second, by practicing relaxing with imagined scenes you will develop your self-control skills to better apply in real life situations. And third, the practice will reduce the power of items on the list to automatically cause undesired responses in you. And this will carry over, in varying amounts, to the corresponding items in the real world.

Most people can profit from the practices with imagined scenes. Some people can reduce or eliminate some causes of anxiety or anger. On the other hand, some people cannot visualize scenes easily or realistically, and for them working with real life situations may be more effective. And for some people the items on their lists produce such strong emotions that this is not an effective or desirable practice. They need to find imagined scenes which produce much weaker responses, and save the other items for later.

## Moving On

You know you have a good foundation in relaxation skills when the following are true: You have developed your own powerful way to relax using breathwork, such as deep breathing and/or 4-2-4-2 breathing. You have used this relaxation practice many times in real life situations. You are continually becoming more aware of bodily cues related to how relaxed you are and changes in this relaxation. You understand and appreciate how concentration, awareness, and breathwork combine to relax body and mind.

## Flexibility II

Increasing mental flexibility increases creativity. Before seeing why that is, begin with two classic exercises that have been used to measure creativity. For each of the following questions spend three minutes (or more if you want) coming up with as many different answers as you can: 1) List all of the uses you can think of for a brick. 2) Suppose all humans were born with six fingers on each hand. List all of the different consequences or implications you can think of.

For an idea to be considered creative it has be original and appropriate. Original means that the idea is unique and unusual, and that the person came up with the idea somewhat spontaneously, not as a result of some set procedure. Appropriate means that the idea meets the requirements of the situation, such as solving a problem or fulfilling some criteria. If when asked how to come up with a cheaper form of energy someone suggests painting all cows blue, that answer would be original but not appropriate.

Consider your answers for uses of a brick. If all of your answers are about building something with bricks, this is not very original. More original answers might include things such as using the brick as a feeding table for squirrels or writing a note on the brick to drop from a boat to an underwater swimmer. What constitutes appropriate could get tricky here. But the general assumption is that the more creative person can generate more unusual uses for the brick.

What were your answers about six fingers? An obvious implication is gloves would need six fingers. Another possibility is that hand slapping would be "high 6" or "give me 6." In mathematics our number system would probably be based on 12 not 10 (twelve fingers versus ten fingers). So in addition to the digits 0–9, there would be totally new single digits for what we call 10 and 11.

Creativity thus involves generating original ideas and deciding which are most appropriate. Developing greater mental flexibility helps in the generating of new ideas. Lateral thinking and being open to making mistakes, learned at the last level, increase mental flexibility and creativity, as does questioning assumptions, learned at this level.

Creativity is also enhanced by seeking out stimulation of new ideas and experiences, such as through reading, the Internet, art, play, travel, clubs, and discussion groups. It is very important that much of this involves direct personal contact with people, such as a book club or church group. And it is very important to spend time in nature.

Nature stimulates all of our senses and helps us get out of verbal linear thinking, which opens us to other ways of perceiving and thinking about specific issues. Nature beckons our awareness and helps us see the bigger more-interconnected picture. Nature provides many examples and metaphors that we can apply to other concerns. For example, how does the metaphor of gardening apply to something you are involved with? Or, consider a plant you observe. What issues does it have growing in that environment? How do the plant's issues of growth compare to your issues of personal growth?

The drunken monkey, who you know doesn't like to be tamed, may try to convince you that you can't become more creative, in general or in specific situations. Watch out for thoughts such as "I'm not creative" or "I don't understand such things." Such thinking is monkey business and should be challenged. You *can* become more creative and you *can* expand your understanding.

The main mental flexibility skill learned at this level is the questioning of assumptions. This questioning includes ideas you have always just assumed were true, but haven't really thought about, and habitual ways of doing things, that you haven't carefully analyzed. Just because you have always thought or acted in some way doesn't mean you have to continue thinking or acting that way. Many people are very reluctant to question and change their ideas or behaviors because it might appear that they were previously wrong. But your level I training should make you more flexible about making mistakes and being wrong.

Some of the most significant and revolutionary discoveries in math and science have come from questioning assumptions. For example, for centuries in Europe it was assumed that the sun revolved around the earth. This assumption made it very difficult to understand astronomical events, such as the movement of the planets. Then scientists started questioning the assumption and suggested an alternate model, where the earth and planets revolve around the sun. This assumption made it much easier to visualize and understand the movement of the planets. Ultimately, one of the assumptions is not more "right" than the other assumption; they are just different point of view or relative frames of reference. But the second assumption—planets revolve around the sun—works better, is simpler, and opened the door for many discoveries.

The same is true for Einstein's revolutionary model and theories. His contributions were based on theories that came from others who questioned basic assumptions of the time, including the best geometry to understand the cosmos and the speed of light relative to an observer. The unquestioned assumptions were questioned and replaced by more useful assumptions. Perhaps in your work the solution to some problem or way to do things better will become apparent when you question some assumption, such as about procedure, direction, or goal.

Although questioning assumptions is good for one's mental flexibility, in practice it can cause problems because it can threaten other people. For example, some of the people who first advocated the view that the earth revolved around the sun were tortured and killed by officials of the church who held to the view that the sun revolved around the earth. Other situations that could be threatening and problematic include teenagers who questions their parents' religious or political beliefs, and the new employee who questions the logic of the company's policy. Question assumptions, but be aware, compassionate, and skillful in how what you say and do may be perceived by others.

Every day your ideas and beliefs strongly affect the way you perceive, think, and act. Almost all of these ideas and beliefs are probably perfectly fine and true in some sense. But there probably are also some ideas and beliefs that are not helpful and true, but you just have been assuming are true. Maybe it is something that a doctor, mechanic, or friend told you, but isn't really true for you. Maybe it is something you believe about another person, but it is based on faulty evidence or misunderstandings.

The key is to be alert to the possibility of a false assumption and to be willing to questions assumptions. Often, the next step is to get the facts. Perhaps you have been doing something based on one doctor's advice, assuming he must know what is right. But maybe the doctor is wrong about you. Get the facts, as by consulting with other doctors and searching the Internet. Perhaps you think someone doesn't like you. You could be wrong. Maybe you misunderstood something that was said. Maybe the person is shy, anxious, or hard of hearing. How would you get the facts in this situation?

Counselors who work with couples are often astonished at the false assumptions between two people who have been in a relationship for years. A common example is that Bob will do something he assumes Marsha likes. Marsha doesn't really like it, but goes along because she thinks it pleases Bob. For years they continue under these false assumptions, without ever discussing it. Or, something that was fun and pleasing to Bob at one time no longer is; yet Marsha continues to assume it is still as it was. Why don't people in relationship talk more and periodically check assumptions about the other person and the relationship? What are some of your unchecked assumptions about someone else, such as a lover, mate, parent, child, or co-worker?

Common examples of unquestioned assumptions come from the roles and labels that cultures teach their members. One is influenced by one's country, neighborhood, family, school, religious group, and television. For teenagers in the United States, assumptions includes the powerful and restrictive influence of cliques, clubs, and gangs. From your culture you learn what it is to be a man or woman, husband or wife, parent or child, and many other roles. The culture socializes you to its values, perceptions, social roles, and lifestyles. Such socialization is fine and natural and a way to help people find their place and get along together. But maybe some of the culturally conditioned assumptions don't apply to you or are harmful in some way. Maybe you have outgrown some of the myths and beliefs that served your earlier. As a student of your own life, it is important that you reflect on some of the assumptions you are making about your social roles. Perhaps you were taught that to be a good boyfriend or husband you must think or act in some way. Perhaps this doesn't apply to you and it is a mistake to assume it does. For example, in the United States it is common for the husband to handle most of the family finances, while in Thailand it is common for the wife to do so. But in both cultures there are exceptions, where the other spouse is better and/or more interested in the task.

Many college students, without questioning what they are doing, pursue a major because it was always assumed by the students' family and/or because it is a popular and trendy major at the time. Thus, a student may be an accounting major because his father is an accountant and it is assumed that the son will be the same and join the family business. This choice often works out well. But many such students find when they are out of college and in their profession that they hate their jobs. For most it will be too late to do anything about it; the responsibilities of their lives limit their choices. Some, at great expense, will quit their jobs and go back to college to study another field. What if these students, while in college, had questioned their assumptions about vocations and learned what really spoke to their hearts?

False assumptions that people make about themselves are common sources of suffering and problems. A person may believe a lot of false things about himself, which makes him anxious or depressed. He should question these assumptions, get the facts, and make friends with himself. Most people limit themselves with false assumptions about what they can or can not do. Many of the drunken monkey's arguments and excuses, discussed throughout this chapter, are based on false assumptions. Becoming more aware of such monkey business alerts you to the need to question assumptions.

One area to question assumptions is conceptual, reconsidering some of your ideas, beliefs, and values. Recognizing the possibility and opportunity for questioning an assumption is the first step. The Mental Play section later begins with a number of puzzles that require you to discover and question assumptions. You might want to do some of them now. But whenever you do them, cultivate awareness of your thinking. Try to notice how your thinking works as you solve the puzzles. Notice assumptions you make.

Other assumptions relate to habitual ways of doing things. Over time everyone develops many habits of daily living. Common examples include the sequence of things one does when one first gets up in the morning, the order in which one reads the parts of the newspaper or checks electronic messages, the exact way in which one washes one's body, the specific route one takes to school or work, where and how one eats lunch, and how one relaxes at the end of the day. Such habits simplify living and free the mind to attend to other things.

However, it is important to be alert to questioning some of these habits. Perhaps by altering a habit you can become more efficient, use different muscles, or add some novelty to your life. Perhaps the technology of dishwashers has changed so that you do not have to rinse the dishes as much before putting them in the machine. Perhaps computer technology has changed so that you can now learn an easier and faster way to complete some tasks.

Just because you have been doing something for a long time does not means you have to keep doing it. Maybe it is no longer appropriate, fun, valuable, or profitable. This questioning also applies to your thinking. Maybe you no longer have to be concerned or worried about certain people or topics. Maybe you no longer need to even have an opinion about some topics.

Letting go of some habits can bring you more freedom, choice, and independence. For example, Marston was a long time reader and subscriber to a particular news magazine. He enjoyed the magazine and felt it was important to be well-informed about political news. However, over time the magazine became an enslaving chore; when the new issue arrived by mail, there was pressure to read it, certainly before the next week's issue arrived. Marston gained a great sense of personal relief and freedom when he realized he did not have to read all or any of an issue of the magazine; sometimes he didn't even open it. For others, freedom may come from realizing one does not have to read the bestsellers one's peers are reading, play the computer games one's friends are addicted to, or follow and participate in current fashions of dressing.

To fulfill the mental flexibility requirements of this level, the following should be true: Rather than just unconsciously wandering through life, as a student you periodically reflect on, and occasionally question, some of your habitual perceptions, thoughts, values, and actions. As a result, you have made some important changes in some of your ideas, and you have found better ways of doing some things. With this has come a greater sense of choice and freedom.

## Learning and Studying

You might find yourself in a situation where you need to study material for some type of exam. The skills that you are developing with this manual will be very helpful. Appendix IV explains this in more detail and adds strategies specifically for studying, learning, and remembering.

This group of practices will reduce studying time and increase memory. Research has shown that college students who utilize these practices significantly improve their grades.

# Mental Play

Here is a continuation of the type of mental play puzzles introduced at the last level. Again, this is not a necessary part of the program—it is just for mental stimulation and fun. So if you don't enjoy such puzzles, don't do them. But if you do play with them, don't give up too easily. They vary from quite easy to very difficult. The first eleven puzzles, numbered 18–28, generally require you to catch a false assumption you are making. The last four puzzles, numbered 29–32, are straight logic problems that can be solved purely by reason; there are no tricks of any type, and they provide all the information you need. For most of the puzzles, there are many possible "right" answers. For a few there is only one right answer. Answers can be found in Appendix III.

18. Two chess players played three games of chess. There were no draws and each player won the same number of games. How can this be?

19. A sheep is tied to a rope. Although the rope is only five feet long, the sheep can get to a pile of hay fifteen feet away. How can the sheep do this?

20. Frank turned off the light in his bedroom and managed to get to bed before the room was dark. If the bed was ten feet from the light switch, how did he do this?

21. "This mynah bird will repeat any word it hears" said the pet shop salesman. A week later the lady who bought the bird was back in the shop to complain the bird had not yet spoken a single word. Yet the salesman told the truth. Explain.

22. Two girls were born on the same day of the same year, have the same mother and father, yet are not twins. Explain.

23. Mr. Smith and his son Arthur were in a car crash that killed the father and injured the son. At the hospital the old surgeon looked at Arthur and said, "I can't operate on him, he is my son!" How do you explain this?

24. As he neared the finish line Tom ran past the others to cross the line first and win the race. Although he wasn't disqualified, Tom did not get the first-prize money. Why not?

25. You are helping a detective friend. From the scene of the crime you follow a set of tire tracks down a little used muddy road and into a driveway. On the front porch are four men, none of whom has a car or mud on his boots. You decide that the most likely suspect is Jay, who is the tallest of the four and the only one with red hair. Why Jay?

26. Why are 1993 pennies worth almost twenty dollars?

27. Your boat has a ladder hanging over the side with rungs a foot apart. At high tide the third rung is just below water level. If the tide falls one foot, how many rungs are out of the water?

28. A three-volume set of books is standing on a bookcase in the usual way. A bookworm starts at the first page of the first volume and burrows by the shortest route to the last page of the third volume. If the pages of each book are one inch thick and each cover is 1/8 inch, how far does the bookworm travel?

29. A bear left his den and went due south in a straight line for one mile. Then he made a 90-degree turn to the left and walked another mile in a straight line. Twice more he made 90-degree turns to the left and walked a mile in a straight line, thus returning to his den. On reaching this starting point, the bear was facing due south. What is the color of the bear?

30. You and two friends are taken into a room where you are all blindfolded. Each of you has a circle put on your forehead, either red or black. You are all given two instructions for when the blindfolds will be removed. First is to try right away to logically determine the color of your circle. (There is no way

to see it and no one will tell you.) Second, if you see a black circle on someone else, raise your hand. The blindfolds are removed, you see two black circles, and everyone raises a hand. After a few minutes you figure out the color of your circle. What is it and how do you know?

31. A woman lives in a cabin with no electricity, computer, phone, TV, or radio. Her clock's battery had run down so she lost track of the time. One day she went to visit a friend, spent the afternoon with him, and then went home and set her clock to the right time. How could she do this without knowing beforehand the length of the trip or how fast she walked? She did not take her clock with her.

32. You have a bag that contains 35 white marbles and 36 black marbles mixed together, plus you have a bowl of additional marbles of both colors. You randomly take two marbles out of the bag and put them in the bowl. If the marbles match in color, two whites or two blacks, a black marble is put in the bag. If they don't match, a white marble is put in. You continue doing this until only one marble is left in the bag. What color is this marble?

# Level III

# WARRIOR

With your student level training, you are now far ahead in terms of being able to use your mind. You know that the practices work and you have profited from them in many ways. You have made good progress in taming the drunken monkey. It might be good for you to remain a student for some time, and gradually add specific warrior level practices as you are ready for them.

But after a while it is time to uplevel what you are doing and become a warrior. This involves more fully bringing your practices and skills into the world, taking firmer control of your life, and standing up to obstacles and problems. The idea of being a warrior with one's life is important in many different cultures, including Native American Indians and Tibetan Buddhists. The term "warrior" as used here is neither male nor female, and does not imply violence or aggression. Rather it is an attitude of taking a strong, active, and responsible approach to living. There are many types of warriors; one might be a peaceful warrior, playful warrior, or silly warrior. If you don't like the word "warrior," pick another term, as long as you develop and maintain the warrior spirit described at this level.

Everyone has a chance to be a warrior from time to time in life. Perhaps one is confronted with a major problem or crisis related to family, job, health, money, or education. Perhaps for ethical reasons one has to take a stand against the group. Most people in such tough situations can be brave and strong and do what needs to be done; they become warriors. A key to effective living is learning to be a warrior in everyday situations, including mental training.

At the novice and student levels the mental training practices are moderately novel for most people, who also start to see the beneficial results of the practices. This helps to keep the practitioner interested and engaged. But this often changes with long-term practice. Some people, as the novelty wears off, abandon the basic practices and seek something new to do. Also, you may periodically hit plateaus in your mental training; you will likely find yourself making steady progress for a while, and then a point usually comes when you get stuck for a while. Not to worry! While the drunken monkey will provide plenty of reasons to justify stopping or switching to something very different, as long as you maintain your dedication and continue your practice you will work through the plateau.

The warrior, however, takes "act with intention" to a new level of commitment, staying with the practices despite impatience, frustration, boredom, and monkey business. The warrior stands strong and simply does the practices, because this is what should be done. There need not be any great dilemma or melodrama here—you simply do it.

Warriors readily take on the problems of daily living instead of running away from them, and they find that the mental training helps them in various ways with these problems. For novices and students, life is divided into doing practices and normal existence. But warriors realize that almost every instant of living is an opportunity to apply or further develop a mental skill. Perhaps it is a time to concentrate one's attention, be more aware of one's feelings, or question an assumption. There is always something mentally that can be done, and the warrior understands the importance of this truth. Training at the warrior level builds on this.

## Concentration III

Breathing has been the major focus of attention as you worked on developing concentration. Breath as an object of concentration should always be part of your practice. Sometimes you will formally spend time cultivating concentration, using the breath as an object. Sometimes in the middle of your day you will notice your mind is restless and unfocused, so you will take just a couple of minutes to quiet and focus your mind by concentrating on your breathing.

At the last level, you added to breathing some additional objects to focus on during concentration training, such as music or body feelings. (You might profit from reviewing the student level instructions about this.) Now, at least once a day you want to identify another situation where you can develop concentration.

For example, you might be at the movies and recognize this as a good time and place to cultivate concentration. First, there are all the external distractions, such as people talking and eating. Whenever one of these catches your attention, you gently and firmly bring your attention back to the movie. Second, there are all the internal distractions, including thoughts, memories, and plans. When one of these occurs, notice it and return to the movie. Thoughts about the movie may be particularly tricky or seductive.

Sports is another good opportunity to develop concentration. The playing of most sports is improved with concentration. This concentration includes staying focused on the task, such as keeping your eye on the ball, and not being distracted by external sights or sounds, such as other players or crowd noise. It involves being focused on the here and now of the sport and not being distracted by thoughts, such as related to winning and losing. What sports or similar activities do you do that would be improved by better concentration? Exactly what will you do to improve concentration in these activities? What might you say to yourself during the activity to remind or guide your concentration development?

Perhaps sometimes you are an artist, such as a photographer or painter. Here you often can use concentration to fully immerse yourself in your creation. You don't want to be distracted by things going on around you. You also don't want your creativity to be limited by monkey chatter in your head, such as thoughts about how your creation "should" come out or what people may think of it. You can think about and evaluate your creation later, not while you are creating. Concentration keeps you from being distracted, helps get your self out of the way, and allows the creative spirit to naturally flow through you.

Listening to other people is definitely an area where you want to cultivate concentration! When someone is talking to you, stay focused on hearing what is being said. When your mind runs off, gently and firmly bring it back to listening. The major trap is being distracted by thoughts about what you are hearing. These thoughts may lead to emotions which further distract you and/or to mental planning and rehearsal of what you are going to say. Try to stay focused on simply listening, you can think about it later. Also, you don't have to immediately react or respond to what you hear; it may be better to reflect on it first. In some cases this will keep you from impulsively doing or saying something you later regret. And listen to hear something new, not just to confirm what you already think.

Fully listening to another person is often one of the greatest gifts you can give, people want to be truly heard. Spouses, children, and workers often complain that others are not listening to them. Whom do you know that might think this way? Note that listening does not necessarily mean agreeing, but first you must listen. Often when people have suffered a crisis, they simply want to tell their story and be heard, they aren't necessarily looking for a solution or cure. Can you sit back, listen, and open your heart? Try to think, see, and feel from the other person's point of view. However, don't be too obviously intense in your listening. If you sit quietly staring at people while they talk you might upset them, and in some cultures this would be too aggressive. Stay concentrated on what they are saying, but let your eyes periodically move around. And periodically say things to show you are listening, such as "Wonderful," "I understand," "I am sorry that happened," or "Why do people do that?"

Concentration training at this level begins with finding at least one situation each day where you can cultivate concentration. Once you are comfortable with this, then look for several situations each day. Freely repeat situations that are common or important, such as listening to people. But variety is also important; continually look for new situations. Eventually you should be easily doing this many times a day, usually without much effort. Also, be aware of when you need to quiet your mind and relax.

To become a warrior relative to concentration is to act on the understanding that basically any situation is an opportunity to utilize and/or develop concentration skills. Warriors are generally aware of how focused and calm their minds are, and increase concentration when needed. Warriors automatically focus their minds when distractions arise. And warriors stop monkey chatter and internal dialogue that would keep them from being fully in tune with reality. Because of concentration, warriors live much more in the here and now.

Most people periodically are involved in multitasking, doing more than one thing at a time. This is not a problem when the tasks are simple or automatic and don't compete with each other, such as housecleaning and listening to music. Unfortunately, more and more people are trying to multitask complex mental activities, such as talking on the phone while driving or doing email. The belief is that such multitasking makes one more efficient. But it is often the opposite, making people less efficient and requiring more time. In addition, the multitasking often causes stress. For complex mental tasks, it is usually best to do them one at a time with full concentration.

## Moment-to-Moment Concentration

As your awareness, development, and use of concentration become fairly regular, you will better understand moment-to-moment concentration (MTMC), introduced in the last level. Even when your mind is only on an object very briefly, your mind can be focused or not. So there are two levels of concentration. One is keeping your mind focused on one object or set of objects. The second level is keeping your mind focused instant by instant, as your mind moves from object to object. This second form of concentration is MTMC. The warrior has direct awareness and experience of MTMC and works at maintaining it.

Sometimes it may seem as if you are aware of many things at the same time. Some people talk about this in terms of "expanding consciousness." But usually it is a case of the mind jumping quickly from one thing to another. Because this jumping happens so fast, it creates the illusion that one is aware of all the things at once. A warrior with advanced awareness of concentration, including MTMC, would see what is actually happening.

## Awareness III

Concentration training at the warrior level involves bringing concentration more fully into daily living and developing and applying concentration more and more. The same is true for awareness training at this level. First you will learn how to be more aware during common activities, such as eating a meal or washing dishes. Then you will gradually apply this training to more and more activities, continually becoming more aware. This training will be a lot of fun and will bring more pleasure into your life. In addition, you will further refine your awareness during your way of practice, such as sitting quietly and watching your breath.

Here are the general guidelines for becoming more aware during activities of daily living. (You should periodically review these guidelines.) First, create the time and space to do just the one activity. Do not combine or multitask it with other activities. For example, eat a meal quietly by yourself—don't combine it with communicating in any way with others, watching television, or reading. Second, do the activity slowly. Take your time, be aware, and enjoy. Eat the meal slowly, noticing all the sensations in great detail. Later you can develop awareness of activities at normal speed and in the midst of other activities. Keep it simple and do it slowly at first. Don't be concerned with what the activity may eventually accomplish. Enjoy the activity for itself in the here and now. Use your concentration to stay focused on the activity.

When cultivating awareness, try to experience things as if they were totally new. When eating, smell and taste as if you have never smelled or tasted anything before. Imagine that you have not had the sense of hearing before, perhaps because you were born deaf or are just now inhabiting a human body. Then, all of a sudden you have the sense of hearing. Try to hear things with this freshness, as if all hearing were new to you. You should take this same approach with all of your senses during awareness training.

Begin the training by eating a meal with increased awareness, slowly and by yourself. First, just look at the food as if you have never seen anything like this before. Notice all the shapes, textures, and colors. Enjoy seeing all the details. Then take a piece of the food and slowly bring it to your mouth. Notice in detail all the feelings in your hand and arm as you do this. Notice the dramatic change in what you see as the food comes toward your face. Notice in detail the smell of the food as it nears your nose and enters your mouth. Experience smelling as if you have never had this sense before. Notice in detail the feeling from your jaws and tongue as you chew the food and move it around in your mouth. Notice the different tastes that occur at different times and in different places in your mouth. Notice the experiences of salivating and swallowing. Continue like this with each bite of the meal until you are aware you have had enough. And throughout all of this: have fun!

Later, if you handwash the dishes, you have another opportunity for awareness training. Here you have a chance to feel in detail water temperature, soap bubbles, and the washing movements of hands and arms. You see in detail the changes in water, soap, and dishes. You are aware of when the monkey runs off, and you notice the change as you bring your mind back to dish washing.

Every day pick at least one activity to do with such full awareness and concentration. Eating a meal is a good place to start. After that pick a wide range of different activities, such as preparing a meal, showering or bathing, putting on make-up, walking, exercising, petting a pet, caressing and being caressed by a lover, doing some task in yard or garden, or playing music. Sit with a friend and see and hear her or him as if for the first time.

Finally, if the activity is something you tend to do in the same way each time, such as brushing your teeth, then consciously change one or more parts of the routine. For example, you might use the opposite hand to brush your teeth or squeeze the toothpaste. You might eat a meal with chopsticks rather than silverware, or the other way around. Change the order and/or way you do your physical exercises. When showering or bathing, clean your body with the opposite hand.

Getting out in nature with some regularity is very important for many reasons, including getting sun and fresh air, clearing your mind, and regrounding yourself. Nature is also a wonderful place to cultivate awareness. This awareness includes sounds of birds, insects, moving water, and wind in the trees; feelings on the body of sun, wind, and grass; and an incredible blend of changing sights. Awareness might be cultivated while silently sitting or slowly walking, perhaps barefoot.

After doing one activity a day for a while, gradually increase the number each day so eventually you are doing awareness training with several activities each day. Then, after you have been doing that for a while, set aside a half day in which you try to do everything will full awareness. This will be a good practice for many years: every now and then set aside a half day or full day to slowly and quietly do everything with great awareness.

As a result of doing the above practices you will gradually become more aware of everything you do, not just the activities you choose for training. You are becoming more and more aware in a very basic sense, independent of what you might be aware of at any time. This awareness leads to the ultimate warrior understanding of awareness training. Just about any situation that you are in or any activity you are doing is an opportunity to cultivate awareness. Warriors learn to be aware of how aware they are at any time, and to actively increase awareness when needed or desired. The warrior's goal is to be as aware as possible as often as possible. One aid is to periodically add in some cue to remind you to be more aware. This cue might be a ring or bracelet that you occasionally wear. Then whenever you notice it, it reminds you to be more aware of what you are doing. Other possible reminders are notes you put in your home, car, or office, or an electronic tone, such as from a timer downloaded from the Internet.

## Awareness of Pain

Pain is an unfortunate part of many peoples' lives. In addition to being unpleasant, pain also readily pulls one's attention to it. Doctors often recommend to people in pain that they distract themselves from the pain by putting their attention on something else. But this seldom works well because most people do not have the concentration skills to override the pull of the pain. On the other hand, exploring the pain with great awareness often helps to reduce the overall aversiveness to pain. So in addition to other things you do to reduce pain, such as drugs, herbs, massage, and acupuncture, try exploring your pain with awareness. Exactly how does the pain feel? Is it dull, sharp, continuous, irregular? How would describe or draw the pain? How do you feel different parts of your body responding to the pain? What thoughts does the pain cause? How do these thoughts affect your body? Separate yourself from the pain so that you are an observer. The pain is not part of the essence of you.

When you actively explore pain and its results in this way, you will probably make a number of discoveries. Perhaps the pain causes you to tense parts of your body in ways that make the pain worse. Perhaps you hold your breath or breathe poorly, when deep breathing might be better. Probably you will have worrisome or anxious thoughts about the pain, which increases your overall suffering. As you become aware of such things, you apply skills you have learned. You might relax parts of your body, breathe relaxing and healing energy into the pain, or stop undesired thoughts. These in turn will reduce the overall suffering triggered by the pain.

An advantage of pain is that it brings one into the here and now of direct experience. For the warrior this is an opportunity for advanced awareness training. First, notice the experience of being fully in the here and now. Notice the quality of this state of being. It may seem cleaner, fresher, simpler, more alive, or more direct. Learn to be aware of how much you are in the here and now at any time. Second, try to bring your awareness to the simple sensation of pain, the pure sensation before you label it "pain" or respond to it in any way. Bring your awareness to the direct contact with the sensation. Notice how this contact leads to feeling, in this case pain, which leads to a variety of thoughts and reactions. This is an advanced practice, so don't be concerned if currently you can only do pieces of it.

## Sitting Practice

In addition to cultivating awareness during daily activities, it is also important to continue to develop awareness during your way of practice, such as sitting and watching your breath. For it is in this situation that you can further hone your awareness, making it sharper and more precise. At this level you will continue the practices begun at the student level; it would be useful now to review the student instructions.

In this practice you sit or lie quietly and put your attention on your breathing. While doing this you will notice various background sensations, such as sounds and feelings. Notice them clearly and stay with your breathing. When a strong sensation arises, let your attention go there and make that the focus of attention, exploring this sensation with focused awareness. The experience might be a sound, thought, feeling, or emotion, among other things. When one of these is the focus of attention, you observe it clearly, experience it in detail, and watch it change. When this object loses its power to pull your attention, or if the object is too unpleasant, bring your attention back to your breathing.

At the student level you learned the optional use of labels for what you are observing. Thus, when a thought arises, you gently in the back of your mind whisper "thinking." The other five basic labels are "hearing," "seeing," "feeling," "smelling," and "tasting." You would not label every sensation that touches your awareness, but certainly any that you attend to, as discussed in the previous paragraph. Experiment with the use of labels during your way of practice or any other awareness training.

Freely make up and add other labels that particularly suit you. If you worry a lot, you might want to use the label "worrying." Other labels mentioned previously include "planning" and "intending." Learning to notice intentions can be very powerful for self-control. Since intentions usually precede actions, being aware of intentions allows you to stop actions that you don't want. Other possible labels include "wanting," "moving," "scratching," and emotions such as "anger," "joy," "happiness," and "boredom."

To further refine awareness during your way of practice, notice how your body and mind interact. Notice how feelings in your body cause thoughts to occur. And notice how thoughts affect your body. Discomfort in your body may produce thoughts of concern. Conversely, unpleasant thoughts may cause tension in part of the body. Put your attention on one of your arms and think about moving it, but don't move it. Notice how just the intention to move creates changes in feelings in your arm. This practice is best done when you are quite relaxed and aware.

The second practice to further refine awareness focuses on the rising and falling of events in your consciousness. Whenever anything comes into your awareness, such as a thought or a feeling, first it arises in consciousness, then it passes through consciousness, and then it falls out of consciousness. Try to be aware of the rising and/or falling of events in and out of your mind. Some people can notice the rising, but have trouble noticing the falling. For other people it is the opposite. Notice what you can.

## Awareness While Walking

So far, your way of practice has emphasized the form of sitting or perhaps periodically lying. Now the form of walking will be added. You can cultivate concentration and awareness while walking in the same way you cultivated them during sitting. The walking can be done at any speed, but at first and periodically it is best to do it slowly.

For slow formal walking, have a walking path of about ten to fifteen yards/meters long. This walking could be inside or outside, wearing shoes or barefoot. Start by standing in a balanced position with your attention on your breath. Clasp your hands lightly in front or back, or let your arms hang at your sides. At first, keep your eyes open, looking at the ground about a yard/meter in front of you. Then just slowly walk with your attention on the feelings of walking, such as the feelings of the ground on your feet and the moving of your legs. Cultivate awareness as described in this whole awareness section. Concentration is developed by continually bringing your attention back to walking. When you get to the end of your path, stop, slowly turn, and walk back. Continue walking back and forth. At first do this for at least ten to fifteen minutes, and then gradually add more time.

Experiment with the use of labels while walking. Gently in the back of your mind whisper "lifting" while lifting a foot, "moving" as you move the foot forward, and "placing" as you put the foot down. Other possible labels include "standing," "intending," "stopping," and "turning."

Some days, such as when you are sleepy, you may find that walking is a better form than sitting. And other days, such as when you are agitated, sitting may be better than walking. Find what works best for you at different times. If you are going to do mental training for a long period of time, as is good to periodically do, then alternate sitting and walking. For example, you might sit for half an hour, then walk for twenty minutes, then sit again, and so forth.

Slow walking is always good, but walking at other speeds can also be good for mental training. Walking might be a slow stroll through yard or park, a brisk walk down the street, or a fast walk for aerobic exercise. Enjoy the walking as a pleasant activity in itself. Be appreciative that you can walk and enjoy the feelings of your feet and legs.

While walking, periodically put your attention on your breathing. When walking quickly, try counting the number of steps you take for each full breath. When walking slowly, try coordinating your breathing and walking. For example, breathe in while lifting your foot, and breathe out while placing it. Or, breathe in during one step, and out during the next step. In either case, breathe naturally and let the breathing determine the rate of walking.

As your warrior training of awareness continues, you will discover many advantages in your life. You will have more pleasure and less fear. You will have better bodily health as you become more aware of your body and influences on your body, such as breathing and stress. You will have more freedom and control over your actions, feelings, and thoughts. You will have fewer accidents, forget less, and won't need to double check things as often (Did I turn off the stove, lock the door, put the cat out, etc?). You will gradually discover true peace of mind. And you will create the space for important insights about yourself.

## Attitude III

Continue to reflect on the four aspects of attitudes that were introduced at the first two levels: have fun, act with intention, make friends with yourself, and be in the here and now.

The warrior sees how these are applicable to all of living, not just mental training.

Have fun. The warrior appreciates the importance of taking control of personal life issues. But this doesn't mean that you can't also have fun while doing important things. Don't add unnecessary seriousness or melodrama to what you do. Just simply do it and have fun. Be open to laughing at yourself when you mess up or are wrong. Be a person that your friends and coworkers have fun being with. Continually look for new ways to add fun into your life and the lives of family and friends.

Act with intention. Whatever needs to be done, simply do it. Don't make a big deal of it. Don't make it more difficult. Don't postpone what should be done now. Don't waste time dreading what you must do. Don't let the drunken monkey talk you out of doing what should be done. And gradually become more selfless in what you do. That is, do something because it is what should be done, not because it will feed your ego, promote your image, or make you appear better than someone else. The warrior is motivated by appropriateness and compassion, doing what needs to be done with an open heart, attuned to the needs and desires of others. Sometimes this will involve helping or serving others, which should be done because it is appropriate, not because it pleases the ego. Selfless service for others is one of the most important things you can do—it will positively transform you and those you help.

Make friends with yourself. Periodically you will be wrong, impatient, closed-minded, and other such things. Periodically you won't be fun, won't do what needs to be done, or will do things just to promote your ego. This is all part of being human, so accept this. Warriors recognize when they are acting inappropriately and try to right themselves as quickly as possible. Warriors take responsibility for what they do and learn from their mistakes. But while you are doing all of this, make friends with yourself. As long as you are learning and growing, don't be too hard on yourself. Love yourself as a person who is doing his or her best.

Be in the here and now. The past is gone, and whatever happened to you in the past is over. Past events may have affected how you think and feel now. If this is true and there are problems, deal with your thoughts and feelings as they are now. Don't allow yourself to be bound by things that happened in the past that you can't change. Be here now. Don't use the past to excuse current problems and misbehavior; you can only be here now. What are you going to do now? Similarly, don't dwell too much in the future. Although it is necessary to do a certain amount of planning for and anticipating the future, most people spend too much time lost in these imaginary places, which usually results in lot of unnecessary worry and anxiety. Be more in the here and now. The drunken monkey lives in the past and future— you want to live in the here and now.

Many people spend much time just preparing to live. They are getting ready for the future and are not living in the present. They are continually involved in various tasks and projects they feel they need to complete before they can turn to the activities they consider most personally valuable and/ or fun. Most people must work in order to play, but work will easily fill up all of one's time if one lets it. One person considers quality time with his children to be very important, but he doesn't get around to it very often because he feels there are other things he needs to do first. Another person puts off many things she wants to do until she retires. The warrior lives by priorities, being sure to build in time and space for those things that are most important. Be in the here and now with your important activities and people, and have fun!

Pets are good teachers for being in the here and now. A dog is asleep on the bed and is then put outside. The dog spends no time reflecting on the bed or wishing he were still there, nor does he get lost in fantasies about being back on the bed in the future. Rather, as soon as he is outside, the dog is in the here and now of that space and seeks what to do now in the outside.

The more you are in the here and now, the more you will realize there is only the here and now. Previously when you had a memory, you were pulled into and lost in this mind space. But gradually you aren't so readily lost and you find yourself in the present having a memory. Similarly with the future. Previously you would get lost in imaginings of the future, but now you gradually stay in the here and now, which includes periodic thoughts about the future occurring in the here and now. If you don't yet understand these distinctions, don't be concerned, you eventually will, as your concentration and awareness increase.

A simple practice to help you be more in the here and now is to mentally comment on what you are doing using the word "now." For example: "Now I am brushing my teeth." "Now I am starting the car." "Now I am worrying about my work."

## Time-Outs

It is very important to periodically take time-outs from what you are doing and relax and reflect. If you are always immersed in your work, family, and other regular activities, you will gradually lose perspective and mental flexibility and probably increase stress. It is necessary to periodically put your life on hold and step out for a while. A time-out might involve going for a walk, sitting quietly, or listening to music. Mental training practice is an important part of this. During time-outs you try to get some distance and perspective on your life, using mental flexibility skills to see things in new ways. These are also times to relax, have fun, and make friends with yourself.

In addition, a weekly day of rest is important to reduce stress and promote the health of body, mind, and spirit. It is a good opportunity to spend time with friends and relatives and engage in playful activities. For religious and spiritual people, it is also a time to attend religious functions, read spiritual works, and pray and/or meditate.

In addition to periodic time-outs and days of rest, it can be very helpful to occasionally go off on a retreat. Here you go somewhere by yourself to get out of your life as fully as possible. You might go camping, house-sitting, or stay at a hotel/motel. The idea is to have a lot of alone quiet time for a few days or more. This is a time for long intense periods of the practices you have learned in this book, plus a small amount of inspirational reading. Formal retreat centers may provide additional instruction and practices. During such retreats you can accomplish things with your practices that are harder to reach in daily shorter practices. For example, during a retreat you might get to deep levels of calmness and/or clarity of mind. Once you have experienced these levels during a retreat, it is easier to reach these levels again during regular daily practices. Such retreats are often a time of personal discoveries and insights, such as occur during Native American Indian vision quests. Warriors recognize the value of such retreats and create the space and opportunity for them.

## Breathwork III

The breathwork skills you learned at levels I and II are all you need for basic mental training. Now you will learn some optional practices, one or more of which might may be help-ful for the health of your body and further quieting or ener-gizing your mind. These practices all come from pranayama, the yogic science of breath. As with all breathwork, remem-ber that if you ever get dizzy, stop the practice and alter it to better suit you. And if you have breathing or heart problems, check with your health advisor about these practices.

## Purifying Breath

This type of breathing helps clean out the lungs. Inhale fully with a deep breath and then exhale most of the air. At the end of the exhale, stop, then exhale a little more, stop, exhale a little more, stop, exhale a little more...Do this until you can't exhale any more. All of this is one purifying breath. Do three purifying breaths in a row.

## Vitalic Breath

This breathing helps clean and strengthen the lungs. First, breathe in through the nose with a series of sharp sniffs until the lungs are completely full. Then, blow out sharply through the mouth with a loud "HAAA." Do this vitalic breath three times in a row. Notice warm feelings in your body, such as your face.

## Alternate Nostril Breathing

This breathing will help you relax and center, quiet your mind, and balance energies. The practice consists of breath-ing through one nostril at a time. This is accomplished by using a finger to push on the side of the nose to close the nostril. Then you alternate back and forth between the two nostrils. In addition, when holding your breath, you pinch both nostrils closed. This practice is usually best done sitting up straight, head straight, eyes closed, and breathing slowly. The complete alternate nostril breathing consists of this cycle:

- Slowly take a deep breath inhaling through your left nostril for a count of 4.

- Hold your breath for a count of 4.

- Slowly and completely exhale through your right nostril for a count of 8.

- Slowly and deeply inhale through your right nostril for a count of 4.

- Hold for a count of 4.

- Slowly and completely exhale through your left nostril for a count of 8.

Do five to ten of these cycles of alternate nostril breathing, pausing between each cycle, while letting your breathing flow naturally.

During all breathwork practices use your concentration skills to keep your attention on your breathing. And cultivate awareness by noticing changes in your breathing and resulting changes in your body and mind.

# Flexibility III

The drunken monkey has a strong tendency to crave and cling to certain things, including sensory experiences, such as wanting to see or hear something in particular. Perhaps a person craves a certain television show or craves pornography. Or perhaps a person craves country music in the car or compliments from others. The mind also clings to specific assumptions and ways of thinking. Hence the need for practices of the previous levels, including lateral thinking and questioning assumptions. And the mind also clings to views of oneself and the world. Thus, people often have trouble changing and growing because they cling to inaccurate or outdated images of themselves. If a person clings to an image of himself as someone who dislikes classical music, always has an expensive car, or can't understand the newest computer technology, then this person will have trouble changing in those areas when change is desirable or necessary.

This craving and clinging creates what is called an "attachment." Attachments are obstacles to mental flexibility, opening the heart, personal and spiritual growth, peace of mind, and freedom. Attachments often create a demand to be satisfied. When not satisfied, one experiences some undesired emotion such as frustration, boredom, anger, or jealousy. Attachments often result in distorted perceptions, since one sees reality as one wants, demands, or fears it to be, rather than how it actually is. And attachments use up a lot energy.

There need not be any problem in having desires and preferences. But when one adds attachments on top of these, the problems begin. For example, consider someone who likes to jog outside every morning before work. Jogging is fine and probably helps the health of body and mind. But if he becomes attached to this jogging and has to have it, then he will suffer when he can't jog, such as when the weather forbids it, he has to go to work early, or family concerns interfere.

Attachments are always bad, even if what one is attached to is good or bad for various reasons. Jogging is often good; attachment to always jogging is bad. Or, consider money: having a job that doesn't harm people in order to earn money is fine, as is earning enough for an appropriate and necessary lifestyle. But if one becomes attached to money, there are many possible problems. One will probably worry a lot more about money. One may spend too much time earning money, rather than more important things, such as being with loved ones. And one will probably perceive more threats to one's money than actually exist.

In yogic psychology it is understood that most attachments fall in one or more of three categories: security, sensation, and power. Security attachments are often related to one's possessions, home, or money. One might be overly concerned about the security of one's home and perhaps think about or perceive threats which are exaggerated or unreal. One might have security attachments to one's self-image and thus be overly concerned about others' opinions of oneself or feel the need to often explain oneself. One might have security attachments to a relationship with another, such as one's child or lover. These attachments might keep one from allowing the relationship to grow and evolve, change being perceived as a threat.

Sensation attachments are related to sensory experiences, such as someone who overeats because of a craving for the pleasure of food, or someone who continually demands more sexual variety. Many people hope to find happiness by accumulating more and more sensory experiences. But although adding pleasure to one's life is often a good thing to do, one won't find happiness by being attached to ever more pleasure. More is never enough. People with sensation attachments are particularly vulnerable to boredom. If one demands that things outside oneself keep one interested and entertained, then one will often be bored and suffer.

Power attachments include how one influences people and situations and how, in turn, one is influenced by them. Power attachments are often related to pride, fame, social-political influence, number of friends, particular friends, and money. Politicians, lawyers, and movie stars often have many power attachments. Many world leaders have made serious mistakes when they misperceived threats to their power. And many celebrities are thrown into severe depression and/or bizarre behavior when their fame decreases. Many people with power attachments have an exaggerated sense of self-importance and often degrade others they feel in competition with.

## Discrepancy Situations

A common and easy place to notice attachments is a "discrepancy situation." This phrase refers to a situation in which reality does not fit how you want or expect reality to be. The child or co-worker is not acting how you want, the social event is not going how you planned, or the politicians are not doing what you think they should. Sometimes the discrepancy will spur you into action, such as trying to influence the child or getting involved in the political process. Sometimes the discrepancy will suggest you be more accepting of reality, such as accepting how the social event is going and not being attached to your plans and expectations. But if in addition to the acting and/or accepting, you allow yourself to be upset by the discrepancy, then almost always this is a sign of an attachment, probably related to security, sensation, and/or power. Be aware when a discrepancy causes anxiety, anger, frustration, or jealousy.

When an attachment in a discrepancy situation causes an undesired emotion, you become less effective at dealing with the discrepancy, whether it requires action and/or acceptance. If the child's misbehavior makes you angry, you will probably be less effective at helping the child learn better behaviors. If you are upset because a social evening is not going as you had planned, then you will probably have trouble going with the flow and fully enjoying the evening. If, in addition to having physical pain, you are also upset because you have pain, then the experience of the pain will probably be worse, and you will probably be impaired in learning how to work with the pain. Sometimes people get anxious about being anxious, or angry about being angry, and thus make the emotion worse.

## Reducing Attachments

The three steps to reduce attachments are the three A's: Attitude, Awareness, and Action. Part of attitude is taking delight in discovering attachments, for it gives you a chance to reduce attachments and improve your life. You are grateful for such opportunities. A second part of attitude is making friends with yourself, unconditionally accepting that you have this attachment, even though you are going to do something about it. A good attitude helps you see reality more clearly and discover attachments faster.

Awareness of attachments is a natural continuation of your awareness training. First, notice the results of attachments, such as undesired emotions, distorted perceptions, and impaired thinking. Then explore your mind, going back in time, to see if you can notice the attachment which is the cause. Watch for discrepancy situations, these are very common and give you many opportunities to discover attachments.

Many people find it very helpful to keep an attachments log. As soon as practical after noticing an attachment, write down important components, such as the following: What was the situation? How did you think and act in the situation? What were the results of the attachment? What did you feel (e.g., anger, fear) and how strong was this feeling on a 1–10 scale? And what do you think was the nature of the attachment? Later, when looking at your log, see if you can classify your attachments in terms of security, sensation, and/or power. Some will neatly fall into one of the categories, others will be a combination. Finally, see if you can discover some trends, themes, or patterns to your attachments. For example, you might discover that many are related to power concerns in the workplace or security concerns about a lover. How will you use what you discover in your log to enhance your awareness of attachments?

The third step is action—what you do to reduce the attachment. This is a large topic far beyond the scope of this book. In some cases it involves behavioral self-control skills. Sometimes it involves the assistance of another person, such as a physical trainer, psychologist, or life coach. But relative to mental training, action involves things you are learning in this manual, including relaxing, quieting the mind, lateral thinking, questioning assumptions, being open to making mistakes and being wrong, making friends with yourself, being in the here and now, and having fun.

The following is a very important requirement for all warriors: spend some time identifying a wide range of attachments in your life. It is probably best if you write them down. For several of the important ones, devise a plan of action. Resolve to implement one of the plans soon. Identify those attachments that can be reduced by one or more the practices listed at the end of the last paragraph. Then make a point of applying those practices to those attachments, having fun at the opportunity to playfully further develop your mental skills. Repeat all or parts of the above requirement as often as needed.

Some people avoid the undesired emotions attachments elicit by avoiding people and situations that trigger attachments. As an extreme, one could go live in a mountain cave. But avoiding attachments does not reduce them—they will wait for their time. Being a warrior includes the willingness and desire to be in the world in the midst of attachments, confronting and reducing them. Sometimes this is difficult, but the warrior is up to the challenge. Attachments are the grist for the mill, opportunities for significant personal and spiritual growth. As a general strategy, warriors actively develop thoughts, feelings, and perceptions which are the opposite of the negative ones elicited by attachments. Thus one develops relaxation to offset anxiety, love to offset hate, and joy at others' accomplishments to offset jealousy.

Reducing attachments has many benefits: reduction of negative emotions, more energy, more accurate perceptions, clearer thinking, peace of mind, increased happiness and well-being, and more freedom. Despite the arguments of many drunken monkeys, reducing attachments does not make a person apathetic or unmotivated. Actually the opposite is true: unfettered by attachments, one can more fully and more effectively engage in the world. The average person with many attachments is usually motivated by security, sensation, and power, and is often driven by forces beyond awareness and control. As one reduces attachments, one's life becomes easier and more spontaneous, and one is more motivated by compassion and what is appropriate for the situation.

## Meditation

In this section we will consider how the practices of this manual relate to the world's literature on meditation. This is an optional section that can be skipped without affecting basic practice. If you want to learn more about meditation, see the Resources list at the end of this book.

The practice of meditation consists of four components: form, behaviors of the mind, attitude, and object. Form refers to what one does with one's body while meditating, such as sitting, lying, standing, or walking. Behaviors of the mind refers to the fact that all the major meditation traditions in the world stress the development of concentration and/or awareness. Thus, the training of concentration and awareness in this manual overlaps the mental training in meditation, and some of the practices in this manual were drawn from the meditation literature.

The attitude component of meditation refers to how one approaches the meditation practices. There are many common elements between the optimal meditation attitude and the attitude components of this manual. This includes act with intention, have fun, be in the here and now, and make friends with yourself. At the next level we will add in the extremely important component of not-doing.

The object of meditation refers to what you put your attention on during meditation. The most common object is the breath, as you have already learned about, and this is the best object for most people to begin with. The object of meditation is what determines whether the meditation practice is primarily for healing the body, psychotherapy, religious/spiritual practice, mental training, or something else. In Chinese healing one might meditate on a particular part of the body as a way to bring healing life force (chi) into that area. In yoga one might meditate on a chakra, a center of interaction of consciousness, mind, body, and energy. Which chakra is chosen depends on many things, such as what systems of the body and/or what category of attachments needs to be worked with. (Security, sensation, and power correspond to the first three chakras.) Meditation on chakras can help a form of the life force (kundalini) move more freely through the chakras.

In Western psychotherapy someone might meditate on a person or situation as way to perceive or understand that person or situation better, and as a way to observe one's related reactions. Or, one might meditate on the behavior of a person who has attributes one wishes to cultivate. In order to cultivate compassion, one might meditate on a very compassionate person handling a situation of personal importance. Or, while maintaining a feeling of lovingkindness, one might meditate on people that elicit negative emotions, thereby gradually reducing these emotions and opening one's heart.

Yogis often meditate on a mantra, a sound, word, phrase, or chant that has particular power and/or significance to the yogi. The best known mantra is the sacred syllable *om* (aum) which symbolizes the Divine. Mahatma Gandhi's mantra was *Ram*, one of the manifestations of God. Christians practicing the prayer of the heart might use the mantra "Jesus" or "Lord Jesus Christ, Son of God, have mercy on me." In the spiritual exercises of Saint Ignatius, one meditates on Christian themes (e.g., sin, Satan) and events of Jesus' life. Some Jewish people meditate on portions of the tree of life from the Kabalah, a symbolic synthesis of previously secret teachings.

A Buddhist might meditate on some theme, such as death or the Buddha, or on a mandala, a pictorial representation of aspects of one's mind or the spiritual cosmos. Zen meditation, called *zazen*, often uses the breath as object. Some

Zen practitioners meditate on a mental paradox that can't be solved by the rational mind (a type of koan), such as the well-known "What is the sound of one hand clapping?" Of all the world's meditation traditions, Buddhism has given the most attention to the cultivation of awareness, called mindfulness. Systematic training in mindfulness can be found in the vipassana meditation practices, where *vipassana* means clear seeing in new, varied, and extraordinary ways.

Your training in concentration and awareness will strongly help you in any of the traditions mentioned above, as well as traditions not mentioned, such as Sufi or a particular Native American spiritual path. If you are at the Warrior level, you already have advanced skills for meditation in all of these traditions. Note that there is no general agreement about the meaning of the word "meditation," and it is often used in ways different than described above. For example, in the United States "meditation" often is used to refer to guided imagery or thinking and reflecting. Because of the confusion surrounding the term "meditation," and because many people have strong positive and/or negative feelings to what they think meditation is, meditation was not discussed earlier in this manual. But more important, from the point of view of learning to meditate is to be clear on the nature of the cultivation of concentration and awareness before one becomes lost in the form and object of meditation.

## Mental Play

Play is a critical part of living. Infants will play with their food and other things within reach. Adolescents will play at adult social roles as a way of learning. Play is fun. Small children will run around just for the pleasure of running. But as people "mature," they often lose much of their ability to play. For example, running for some adults is no longer fun—it is now an unpleasant task done for health reasons.

The playful warrior recognizes that having fun is not only pleasurable but also good for the health of body, mind, and spirit. The warrior brings the attitude of having fun to as many activities as possible. The warrior looks for and creates many opportunities to play. And the warrior understands playtime as a time to be in the here and how, a time to be free and open to novelty and surprise, and a time for creativity and lateral thinking.

Games are organized play with rules and objectives. Physically active games, including sports, are ways to develop the body and learn important skills, such as teamwork and sportsmanship. Electronic games might help develop concentration, memory, decision-making, pattern recognition, and hand-eye coordination. Fantasy and role-playing games might stimulate the imagination and creativity. Group/party games can add fun to a social event with people who like games. The Internet is a vast resource for information about games, opportunities to play games against computer programs, and a vehicle to play games with other people, which might be a few people in games such as poker or bridge or many people in a fantasy world. In this book's Resources section are listed some good books of games.

Unfortunately there are some traps that impair healthy game playing, three of which are very important in the United States and elsewhere. First is the large number of adolescents and teenagers who spend too much time with video and computer games at the expense of needed physical activity, fresh air, and social interactions. Second are the people who get lost in and attached to a fantasy role and/or fantasy world at the expense of their personal development in the real world. And third are the people who only have fun if they win. The warrior usually tries to win since that is usually the objective of a game, but the warrior always has fun playing, win or lose.

But our interest here is on games that facilitate mental training and complement the skills you are learning from this manual. Some games develop concentration and memory. The classic example here is the game Concentration, which is played with a deck of cards (see Appendix V), and was the basis for a popular TV game show. A spread-out deck of facedown cards is gradually exposed and players try to remember where specific cards lie.

Many paper and pencil games require logical thinking, such as using trial-and-error plus logical deduction to determine a word (Hangman), positions of ships on a grid (Battleship), or general patterns (Eleusis, Patterns II).

A good example of this type of game is Bulls and Cows (see Appendix VI), which was developed into the very popular game Mastermind. The best known board game of deduction is Clue (also Cluedo), in which one might find a certain character was the culprit using a specific weapon in a particular room. Other deduction games include Sleuth, Black Box, and Orient Express.

There are a large number of strategy games that cultivate many different mental skills. Many excellent games of this type can be played with paper and pencil, a deck of cards, dice, and dominoes. Fun can be had very inexpensively. In addition, there are now many very good strategy board games, some of which are listed in Appendix VII.

When game experts are polled about the world's best non-gambling strategy games, three games are often on the top of the list: chess, Go, and duplicate bridge. For all three there are many books, computer programs, clubs, and tournaments. Chess is well-known, and inexpensive computer programs and computer chess sets play at the expert level and provide instructions and suggestions for the learner. Go is a Chinese game of placing stones on a grid, with just a few rules that can be learned in a few minutes. But these simple rules generate a game with great depth and subtlety. Bridge is arguably the best trick-taking card game. (Some Germans would suggest that their game of Skat is the best such game, or the best for three players.) Many people get stopped by the complexity of bidding in bridge. But once a simple system is learned, it becomes a fun and important part of the game. The "duplicate" variation of bridge, played in many clubs, greatly reduces the luck of the deal by having different people play the same hands. Books about Go and bridge can be found in the Resources.

Most adults need to learn to play more in order to increase pleasure and health. Games are a good way to play. In addition, many games help develop and maintain mental skills, and keep the brain functioning well. Warriors find games that they and various friends enjoy. Most important, warriors enjoy playing with all aspects of living with all of its interesting challenges.

# Level IV

# ADEPT

If you have completed the warrior level, you are now quite advanced in the practices and way ahead of where you began. However, there will always be more to learn; this is one of life's beautiful things. At this level you will learn some advanced practices and perspectives, and you will do more weaving together of what you have learned. You will be on the continual path to become more expert, more adept.

At this level you will come to appreciate more how everything is interrelated. Concentration and awareness were treated as separate skills at first, but by now you realize they are highly interrelated in complex ways—they always influence each other, and changes in one produce changes in the other. Hence, at this level it is usually best to work with them simultaneously. Similarly, concentration and awareness are intertwined with mental flexibility. For example, becoming more aware helps to reduce attachments, and reducing attachments improves the clarity and breadth of awareness. And concentration, awareness, and mental flexibility are all intertwined with attitude and breathing, as you have already discovered and will learn more about. At this level we will add in practices related to opening the heart. Although it is not specifically mental training (the focus of this manual), you will discover how opening the heart is totally intertwined with concentration, awareness, mental flexibility, and breathing. All of these are intertwined with ethical behavior. For example, the more ethical you are, the easier it will be to quiet the mind, reduce attachments, and open the heart. Finally comes the understanding that body, mind, and spirit are all totally intertwined. So the mental training of this manual will improve the health and functioning of the body and spirit as well as the mind. The most advanced understanding of this reality includes how all these are interwoven and affect each other.

A very powerful dynamic at the adept level is readiness to hear, the ability to personally understand in a deep and profound way because of one's life experiences and development. What this means is that the novice, student, and warrior will understand the practices and perspectives of the adept level in very different ways! Because warriors have had extensive experiences and discoveries with the practices, they will understand and appreciate many of the instructions of this level in ways that the novice can not yet understand. A strong example of this is the upcoming discussion of "not-doing." Most people can easily read this section and get something out of it. But the warrior will understand it in a much more profound way, and it will resolve some fundamental concerns. For the importance of not-doing is very pervasive and often very subtle. For example, not-doing is basic to Western control and acceptance therapies, as well as the central practice of philosophical Taoism, an essential Zen approach to meditation, a practical conclusion of Hindu/yogic advaita vedanta, one of the highest teachings of Tibetan Buddhism, and a core revelation of many relatively recent spiritual teachers (e.g., Krishnamurti, Jean Klein, Toni Packer, Adi Da, and Adyashanti).

## Concentration IV

Warrior level training in concentration is sufficient for most people's mental training. Further development at the adept level is based on the understanding that any situation is an opportunity to further refine one's concentration, although this obviously is much easier to do in some situations than others. Thus, every situation is a chance to do one or more of the following: be aware of how concentrated your mind is, actively quiet and focus your mind more, and keep your attention focused. But don't overwhelm or strain yourself here. Be patient and gradually cultivate more and more concentration.

The adept level is also the time to further refine moment-to-moment concentration (MTMC). First, review the discussion of MTMC at the warrior level. Sometimes you will intentionally put your attention on some object, sometimes you will let attention go where it's called to or programmed to go. Sometimes you will hold your attention on some object, sometimes you will just let it go. But in all of these cases you can have strong MTMC, clear concentrated focus on the object of attention, whether your attention stays on that object for just a moment or longer.

As a practice in understanding how concentration and awareness interrelate, read through the questions in the Awareness Questionnaire (Appendix I). For each question, consider how both concentration and awareness apply to what is being asked. In each case, how would a change in concentration affect awareness, and how would a change in awareness affect concentration? From these questions identify areas that would be particularly useful or important for you to simultaneously develop concentration and awareness. This exercise will give you practice combining concentration training and awareness training, and will ensure that in these areas you don't overlook the importance of both types of training.

## Awareness IV

Like concentration, awareness training at the adept level is based on the fact that every situation is an opportunity to develop awareness. For any situation one can do one of more of the following: be aware of how quiet and focused the mind is, be aware of how aware you are of the situation, be aware of related thoughts and feelings, notice any attachments and/or their effects, actively increase concentration and/or awareness, encourage awareness to move into new areas, and encourage awareness to be clearer and sharper. And one can always be aware of one's breathing and one or more of the attitude components.

Relative to your way of practice, there is a simple but advanced way to cultivate awareness. Sit quietly using your breath as the primary object of attention. Once your mind is quiet, focused, and aware, simply be aware of whatever arises in your consciousness. Don't try to keep your attention on any object. Don't try to stay focused. Don't try to be aware. In fact, don't try to do anything! Switch from doing to being. Just simply be in the here and now, noticing whatever arises in your mind. Let your mind go where it wishes, but whenever it is not drawn to something in particular, bring your attention back to your breath. Periodically, as spontaneously feels appropriate, intentionally quiet the mind, choose objects of attention, and/or encourage awareness. At such times, be aware of intending, acting, and any of your "selves" as the actor. Don't try to do or accomplish anything, just be aware. This is a time for not-doing. This is a time for awareness of whatever, a non-time for pure awareness.

Next are two optional mindfulness exercises (*vipassana*) to further hone down awareness. These are not necessary for the program of this manual, but may be useful to some practitioners. They both build on your way of practice. For explanation we will assume you are sitting and watching the rising and falling of your diaphragm, using the labels "rising" and "falling." You can alter these instructions to suit your particular practice.

## Exercise One

Add in noticing sitting, your sensory experience of what it feels like to sit. When noticing the sitting, use the label "sitting." Now, in between noticing the rising and then the falling of the diaphragm (or in between the falling and then the rising), notice the sitting. So your labeling will go: "rising," "sitting," "falling," "rising," "sitting," "falling." Your breathing should be natural and not affected by the practice. If by noticing sitting you lose awareness of rising or falling, you may not yet be ready for this practice.

## Exercise Two

The second practice builds on the first. Now we add in "touching." You pick some touch point in the body, a point about the size of a coin that you can easily feel, such as a point on the right buttock that you feel from sitting. Then you let your mind touch the sensation at this point, feeling not thinking, while labeling "touching." Finally, you insert this into the first practice between falling and rising. So the labeling for the whole practice goes "rising," "sitting," "falling," "touching," "rising" ... Again, if you lose awareness of any component, you may not yet be ready for this. With continued practice you will reach readiness. Later, you can add additional touch points. For example, during "touching" your mind goes to a touch point on the right buttock and then to a touch point on the left buttock, and then to "rising." One can gradually add more and more touch points into this awareness interval, such as touch points in the knee, ankle, or elbow.

Practices such as the above two make one's awareness sharper and faster. It is also a good time to develop MTMC.

## Breathwork IV

With your extensive breathwork practice at previous levels, you have already mastered the necessary basics of good breathing, and you know how to use breathing to relax or energize yourself. Plus, you know how to use breathing as a primary vehicle to cultivate concentration and awareness. At this level we will further refine awareness.

Although you have learned a lot about breathing, this is not the time to start taking it for granted. It is important to stay aware of your breathing. And the adept practitioner appreciates the importance of periodically bringing one's full attention to one's breathing as a means to center, ground one's self, relax, and pull into the here and now! When you are too much in your head, perhaps caught in unpleasant thoughts and/or memories, switch your attention to your breathing. When you are lost in imaginary places of past or future, bring yourself into the here and now of your breathing. When you are mentally agitated and your concentration is poor, quiet your mind by focusing on your breathing. If you feel too spacey or out of touch, ground yourself by concentrating on your breathing. When you want to improve your awareness, observe your breathing.

The main breathwork practice at the adept level is the smoothing out and evening out of breathing. When observing your breathing, notice when and where the breathing is uneven or erratic. Notice if the breathing is sometimes quick or sometimes slow, notice when it is smooth or harsh, and notice if it periodically stops. Gradually guide your breathing into a slow and even rhythm. While observing all the stages of a complete breath, be sure that your breath is evenly distributed throughout your lungs.

Observe the flow of inhalation and exhalation, it should be smooth with no jerking. If not, smooth it out. Don't intentionally inhale or exhale, just let them happen (not doing). Let the breath move evenly on its own. Don't try to inhale, wait for the breath to come to you and receive it gratefully. If you notice that you are gradually increasing the amount of air you are taking in, neither encourage or discourage this. Let your breathing find its own optimal level.

Periodically throughout the day, be aware of your breathing. Notice changes in the nature of your breathing at different times of the day and in various situations. Observe the relationships between your breathing and your emotional states. Notice how your breathing affects your relaxation and energy. Train yourself to instantly notice any dramatic changes in breathing, such as breath holding, increased rate of breathing, or a switch from diaphragm breathing to chest breathing.

As an awareness practice, explore the space between and around your breathing. Put your attention on the conscious space between exhaling and inhaling. That is, after a complete exhalation and before inhalation begins on its own, there is space. Focus on this timeless space. Notice how exhalation and inhalation are processes that arise out of, and occur within, this space. This is the same space that occurs between thoughts. Let yourself merge and become one with this space. At first it might be helpful to visualize this space as being all around you, but eventually let go of any such visualizing. Relax, and settle into the here and now of this space. What is the relationship between this space and your awareness?

## Self Awareness

This section contains a sequence of awareness exercises related to your "self." You will explore that self which is unique to you, not someone else's self or some generic self. You will discover some of your thoughts and feelings about your self, but the emphasis will be on your direct experience of what you consider to be your self. Regardless of anyone's specific thoughts and feelings about her or his specific self, these are powerful awareness training exercises for everyone at the adept level. Some of the exercises are quite simple, others are subtle and profound. All together these practices have the potential to significantly alter the lives of adept practitioners. It is generally best, at first, to do the exercises in order.

1. Who am I? What are your best answers to this classic question about your self? Who do you think you are?

2. What are your thoughts and feelings, positive and negative, about this self? What do you think about your self? How do you feel about your self?

3. Stand in front of a mirror and look at your image as if seeing it for the first time. How does this image relate to you? How does this image define you? How does all this relate to your self?

4. What is your direct first-hand experience of your self? Right now, how do you experience this self?

5. Where does this self live? What is your experience of the location of your self? Perhaps it is inside the head, with a body below. Perhaps it is in the center of the body. Perhaps it completely fills up the body. Perhaps it is outside of the body. Or perhaps it is somewhere else or moves around. Where is your self?

6. How do you experience your self as the observer or witness? Right now you are reading and/or thinking. Right now what is your direct experience of some self that is doing the reading or thinking? Right now you are probably seeing, which includes the object of seeing, the process of seeing, and the self as the observer or seer. What is your immediate experience of this self? Similarly when you are hearing: What is your experience of some self as hearer, as opposed to what you are hearing? If you are confused or troubled by this exercise, then what is your experience of some self that is confused or troubled?

7. How do you experience your self as actor, the willful agent of action? Willfully and slowly do some simple action, such as move a finger. What is your direct experience of the self which wills the action? What is your experience of the process of willing?

Through self-related awareness exercises, such as the above, you will discover an important difference between self as object and self as subject. Self as object refers to the thoughts and feelings you have about yourself, what Western psychologists call self-image, self-concept, and self-esteem. The amount of poor self-concept and low self-esteem varies tremendously among individuals and among cultures. For example, it is a widespread problem for people in the United States, but largely unknown among Tibetans.

If you discover that you have many negative thoughts and feelings about your self, here is what to do: First, realize they are just thoughts and feelings, not the real essence of you. So if the thoughts or feelings are negative or problematic, use your mental skills to stop or replace them. Second, use your mental flexibility skills to question the content of some of your thoughts. Perhaps some of your negative thoughts are based on false assumptions you are making about yourself. Third, don't define yourself in terms of what you used to do—be in the here and now, and define yourself in terms of what you are doing now. Fourth, apply some of the strategies you have learned relative to making friends with yourself. And fifth, freely enlist the help of a professional counselor if you are having particular problems with this. A "humanistic" counselor focuses on these types of issues.

Self as subject refers to your subjective experiences of your self as the perceiver, actor, and witness. It is your experience of yourself as the seer of sights, hearer of sounds, taster of tastes, thinker of thoughts, and doer of actions. Systematically using your awareness skills to look for and explore your self as subject is a powerful and freeing transformative practice. This practice of "self-inquiry" is a central part of some Buddhist and yogic meditations.

A useful form of self-inquiry is applicable to all adept practitioners: Whenever you are pulled into some negative space, such as anger or boredom, practice self-inquiry. For example, if you are angry, then ask yourself "Who is angry?" What is your immediate and direct experience of some self which is angry? This is a powerful practice which will help you learn more about your self, discover self-related attachments, and become more free.

## Flexibility IV

Flexibility at this level focuses on attachments related to the self you just explored. First, review the whole discussion of attachments in Flexibility III. The strategies for reducing attachments discussed there apply to the attachments discussed here. Two major differences are that self-attachments are often subtler and more pervasive than other attachments, and it is often easier to reduce self-attachments using just the skills cultivated through this manual.

You have already uncovered some of the thoughts and feelings you have about your self. There are, of course, more to be discovered. Attachments occur when you cling and hang on to some of these thoughts and feelings, even though they may be causing problems. A lot of human suffering is caused by such self-attachments.

If you are attached to a particular image of yourself, that will probably impair your personal growth. For example, a person who is attached to the image of being consistent may lose mental flexibility when it is desirable to not be consistent and consider other alternatives. Or, a person who is attached to the idea of being compassionate may misperceive a situation where he wasn't compassionate, perceiving himself as having been more compassionate than he actually was. This attachment-caused misperception keeps the person from learning from the situations how to actually be more compassionate. A person addicted to some drug, such as alcohol, may misperceive how addicted he actually is, because he is attached to a self-image that doesn't include drug addiction. You want to cultivate clear awareness of yourself and your behaviors, so make friends with reality as it is, and let go of attachments.

Many people don't like some part of their bodies, such as their hair, nose, or hips. Because the reality of the body part does not match some image of how the person wants it to be, the person suffers. Maybe the person gets anxious when thinking about this body part or seeing it in a mirror. Maybe the person is jealous of someone else's body part. Adepts recognize the unnecessariness of this suffering, change what they can, and make friends with themselves. In addition, comparing oneself with others often produces bad feelings and creates separation from the others.

A person with power attachments related to the self may be too concerned and influenced by the perception of others' opinions. These attachments will impair the person's perception and thinking. Also, you can't please everyone, so if you are attached to everyone liking everything you do, you are bound to suffer. Other people may allow others to abuse them because they believe they don't deserve better.

The more attached a person is to some image of the self, the more the person will protect, defend, and explain this self. For example, if a person is attached to an image of himself as being a smart person, he may be threatened by someone else appearing smart, or he may feel the need to explain why he was actually smart in a situation where he did not appear smart. Also, the more the self-attachments, the more self-centered the person will probably be. Such a person may readily exaggerate his importance.

What the adept comes to realize is that the fundamental nature of a person is clear, sane, loving, complete, and interconnected. But for most people this is covered over by attachments, and people identify with a much inferior self with lots of suffering. So the adept gradually frees her or his true self from the attachments. Remember, you are not your behaviors, what you do, nor are you the contents of your mind. You can change these! You can discover the real nature of your being—the potential is in your hands.

## Attitude IV

The attitude components you have been cultivating for some time now include acting with intention, having fun, being in the here and now, and making friends with yourself. At this level, we add in not-doing. These five approaches to living will always be applicable, and at any particular time, one or more may be very good advice! Periodically pick one of these five attitude components and reflect on how it relates to your life. When are opportunities to apply and cultivate it? Adepts have a profound appreciation for the importance of attitude in general and these five components in specific. Adepts have personally discovered the power, breadth, and subtleties of applying these to their lives, periodically surprised at how there is much more to these effects than they had expected.

Consider some examples related to not-doing: When Max the cat is sleeping on the floor, his human pets can walk right next to him and not disturb him. But one day when one of his humans went to get him for a trip to the vet, Max woke up quickly and took off running. In the human's attempt to be natural in walking toward Max, he actually moved unnaturally and alerted the cat.

Early in his dating, a young teenage boy asks for advice from his mother. She gives the common response, "Just be yourself." But instead, the boy tries to act in a way that fits his image of how an ideal date should act, perhaps trying to imitate a particular peer. The date would have gone better with less such trying and more being himself.

An actor in a comedy makes the mistake of trying to be funny, when it is the situation that is funny if he just behaves naturally. Common advice from skilled actors is don't try to "act," rather simply do what is required in the here and now of the situation with no preconceptions.

In all of these situations, instead of just naturally doing the appropriate thing, the person tries to be spontaneous, tries to be natural, and tries to do what he thinks is appropriate. But this very trying usually makes the person less spontaneous, less natural, and less appropriate. The essence of not-doing is to let go of this unnecessary and often counterproductive trying. You relax into the here and now and simply do what needs to be done without adding unnecessary heaviness and melodrama. For example, as you now know, the practices of this manual can revolutionize your life, so doing the practices is very important and powerful. But when doing the practices the optimal attitude is not heavy and dramatic, rather it is light and playful. You just simply do the practices in the same way you do many other things, such as taking out the trash.

Not-doing often involves getting the limited self out of the way. This little self often wants to be actively involved, on the front line doing things. But this self and its doing often muddle things up. Thus, in order to be spontaneously appropriate, it is sometimes necessary to bypass or suppress this self. Consider two musicians: The first musician consciously and willfully reads the music and plays the instrument. But for the second musician there is no self, the musician and instrument have become one, and music is simply happening.

Not-doing does not mean one should be passive or uncaring. On the contrary, most of us need to be in the world doing things with personal, professional, and social implications. The trick is to keep from imposing on what we do a self-centered melodrama. Simply do it.

Not-doing can help many activities, including interpersonal relationships, sports, and art. It can reduce stress, increase mental flexibility, illuminate the nature of the self and will, and facilitate personal and spiritual growth. Not-doing is very powerful and pervasive, and the beauty is there is nothing to do.

The novice is primarily motivated by security, sensation, and power. And his experience of the world is that much of what he does is by an act of will by his self. The adept, on the other hand, allows the situation to spontaneously bring forth the appropriate action. And he is primarily motivated by compassion and appropriateness.

## Opening the Heart

Like breathwork, opening the heart is not specifically mental training, the central theme of this manual. But opening the heart (again like breathwork) strongly interacts with the mental skills, particularly at the adept level. So it is necessary to briefly consider this important area. Relative to themes of this manual, opening the heart has two basic aspects: openness and unconditional acceptance.

### Openness

Developing openness involves cultivating a welcoming receptivity to thoughts, memories, experiences, and people. It involves allowing more experiences to come into your life and breaking down barriers between you and others. Perhaps there are aspects of yourself that you disown or don't acknowledge. Openness involves recognizing and accepting them, which is accompanied by making friends with yourself and perhaps doing something to improve yourself. Openness to other people may involve dismantling barriers that keep you psychologically separate from others. These barriers might be based on anxiety, anger, jealousy, or specific past experiences. Being open to another person does not mean you have to like him, you might choose to avoid this person, But when any person is with you, it is to your and his advantage for you to be open to this person's thoughts and feelings, so that you can perceive accurately, think clearly, and respond appropriately. And such interpersonal openness increases harmony and decreases stress.

Being open to new ideas, including ones that are contrary to your ideas or beliefs, increases mental flexibility. Such openness facilitates lateral thinking, creativity, and challenging assumptions.

## Unconditional Acceptance

The second aspect of opening the heart is unconditional acceptance, accepting reality as it is, because at the time of acceptance, reality can't be different than it is. This acceptance does not mean that you don't have opinions about some part of reality or that you don't try to change reality.

But while you are doing what you do with the current reality, you accept it as it is. You don't upset yourself because reality is not how you want or expect it to be. For example, Mary is overweight, which is hurting her physically and psychologically. She could deny she has a weight problem and/or stay attached to her image of herself. Or, she could be aware of her weight problem and allow herself to be upset by it. Being upset might motivate her, or it might interfere with attempts to lose weight, or it might lead to depression. But if Mary is a warrior or adept practitioner, then the following can be true: Mary's open awareness allows her to see she is problematically overweight. She unconditionally accepts this because it is true, and she makes friends with herself. She then embarks on a systematic plan to lose weight. As long as she follows her plan or some reasonable revision of it, there is no need for her to be upset with herself. And she does all of this without making it into a melodrama (not-doing).

If you have a child, it is very important that you communicate that you always love her or him unconditionally. That is, no matter what the child does in life, you will always love him and be on his side. However, that does not mean you will always approve of various actions and choices of the child. As a parent, you have a responsibility to influence these behaviors and decisions. Thus, you always unconditionally love the essence of the child, regardless of whether you approve or disapprove of his current behavior. So if your child misbehaves, you don't tell him he is a bad person! You tell him his behavior is unacceptable and has consequences. But he is always a lovable person.

Many people can develop unconditional acceptance for their own children, but what about some non-relative that causes you problems or makes you angry or anxious? The adept cultivates unconditional acceptance for all people, with no exceptions. Acceptance does not mean that you necessarily like a person's behavior. You might try to help him change his behavior, or you might stay away from him. But regardless of any person's behavior, you accept this person unconditionally. For everyone is one of us doing the best he or she can based on his or her experiences, perceptions, values, and understanding.

Acceptance does not mean being passive. If there is something that could and should be done, do it. But whether you can change the situation or not, accept it. What you accept is important, but more important is the accepting itself. Be aware of the pure experience of accepting, regardless of what is being accepted. This is an act of the heart, not the mind. Three practices that help opening the heart are forgiveness, sympathetic joy, and lovingkindness.

Forgiving others for things that happened in the past greatly opens the heart. Forgiveness is not forgetting or condoning bad things that were done to you, and you may still hold the person accountable in some way. Forgiveness does not mean staying in a hopeless situation that is unhealthy. Rather, forgiveness is letting go of negative emotions, bad memories, grudges, and attachments that create barriers and/or a desire for others to suffer or be punished. To forgive others heals oneself and frees the others. If someone hurt you, he is responsible. But if in addition to this, you suffer from thoughts, feelings, and attachments about this person, then you are responsible for this part of the suffering. In addition to forgiving others, it is very important to forgive yourself, make friends with yourself!

Sympathetic joy is taking delight in the successes and accomplishments of others. It is opposite to and offsets jealousy, envy, and begrudging. Working in this area helps you discover many self-related attachments. Maybe Bob got the promotion you hoped for. Maybe this decision was right or wrong in some way. Maybe this will affect what you do next in the workplace. But in the midst of this you take joy in Bob's success, how nice for Bob. And you notice how any of your related anger or jealousy is based on attachments.

Opening the heart increases love, empathy, compassion, and peace of mind. It also reduces attachments and therefore increases mental flexibility. With fewer attachments and more openness, one's awareness naturally expands. All of these changes then make it easier to quiet the mind and concentrate. And all of this reduces stress and increases the health and happiness of body, mind and spirit. The adept understands and appreciates how all of these are holistically interrelated.

# Lovingkindness

As the word suggests, lovingkindness is a wonderful blend of love and kindness. Lovingkindness includes tender regard, compassion, and active good will. It involves friendliness to others and a desire for their happiness and well-being. At its best it means cherishing all beings and seeing the lovability of all beings. Lovingkindness excludes anger, envy, ill-will, and desire for harm to others. Lovingkindness involves generating and sending feelings of love and well-being to other people. It is reflecting on people with an open heart and sincere compassion. A powerful way to learn how to do this is through lovingkindness meditation, as described below. All adept-level practitioners should spend time with various versions of this meditation.

The practices described here are very similar to and compatible with cognitive behavior therapy counterconditioning and Buddhist lovingkindness (*metta*) meditation. In yoga these practices are understood to keep open the fourth and fifth chakras. For Christians the practices provide a practical way to follow Jesus' commandment to love your enemies.

————

Below are described two separate practices, one to do by yourself, and another for group practice. In both you will generate lovingkindness and send it to other people. Once you get the general idea and spirit of these practices, you can devise your own variations and incorporate and combine them with your other practices.

In the individual practice you will start sending lovingkindness to people that you like and then gradually move to people you don't like. Later, you can add people you have strong negative feelings toward, perhaps even hate. Through this practice you open your heart, and you can eventually rid yourself of automatic conditioned negative feelings. This practice includes people who have done something very wrong. As discussed relative to forgiveness, this does not mean forgetting what the person did or not holding the person responsible for what was done. Rather it is a way to free yourself of unnecessary negative feelings that only hurt you.

In the group practice you need someone to lead the group in meditation. This might be someone who is chosen to be the leader for today's practice, or you might play recorded instructions that you created. In the group practice, in addition to sending lovingkindness, you also receive it and learn to open more to grace. Many people dramatically feel the group's lovingkindness, and for some the feeling will last for a while. The group practice is good for meditation groups, therapy groups, personal growth groups, and church groups.

## Loved One

For these practices you need to pick a "loved one," which simply means some being for whom you feel a lot of loving-kindness, and who will be the first on your current hierarchy, discussed below. This being, currently alive or not, could be a relative, such as a child, sibling, parent, or grandparent. It could be a lover, spouse, and/or good friend. Your loved one could be an animal friend, such as a dog, cat, or horse. Or, it could be a religious figure, such as Jesus, Krishna, or a guru.

In choosing a loved one for this exercise you want to pick a being for whom you feel love, kindness, and compassion and who probably feels these toward you. Note that the way you demonstrate lovingkindness toward this being may or may not be how this being demonstrates lovingkindness toward you. An animal friend is a good example of this. Second, for these practices you should pick a loved one who does not also elicit any strong negative feelings, such as grief. Such a person can occur later in your hierarchy.

## Generating Lovingkindness

The next component of the practices is having ways to generate feelings of lovingkindness. First, create the time and space for doing these practices, as you learned long ago for your mental practice. Second, add to your practice area any music, pictures, smells, or other cues that help elicit loving-kindness. Third, relax body and mind with the techniques you have learned, such as muscle relaxation, breathwork, and concentration.

Next, you need to develop your own particular ways to bring forth lovingkindness. One way is to meditate or reflect on images related to lovingkindness, such as your loved one and other people. You might imagine someone doing something very lovingly or with great compassion, perhaps to you or some other being. You might imagine someone doing something that elicits lovingkindness in you, such as your spouse feeding the baby or your lover crying at the movies. You might remember a wedding or a birth.

You might add speech to what you imagine, such as something you remember Grandma saying or a quote from Jesus. Make a list of words that to you are related to lovingkindness and incorporate them into your scenes and/or just periodically say some of the words while generating lovingkindness. Possible words include the following: sweet, cute, dear, gentle, kind, tender, precious, beloved, heartfelt, genuine, acceptance, sincere, vulnerable, reflective, embrace, and smile.

During all the above use your concentration skills to stay in the here and now focused on lovingkindness. In addition, it is very important that you cultivate awareness of exactly what it feels like to be in the "space" of lovingkindness. This will help you more quickly return to this space and notice what pulls you out of the space and what helps you get back in. Eventually you want to be regularly aware of the amount of lovingkindness you have during your daily living.

## Hierarchy

For the individual practice you need to create a hierarchy, a listing of beings ranked in terms of current feelings of lovingkindness. Over time you will alter this hierarchy, add new items, and create all new hierarchies.

For your first hierarchy, have about ten beings on the list, although feel free to have a few more or less. The first being on your hierarchy is your loved one, discussed above. Second is someone you like a lot, and third is someone you like, but less than the second person. Your hierarchy then progresses through people you like less and less, to people you are neutral about, to people you dislike. For your first hierarchy end with someone you moderately dislike. Later you can gradually add people whom you strongly dislike.

It is important that the hierarchy is gradual, there is not a big emotional jump from one item to the next. Thus, you do not want to go from a person you like a lot immediately to someone you dislike a lot. Alter and add to your hierarchy so the transitions are gradual and smooth.

## Individual Practice

Generate feelings of lovingkindness. Then meditate on the first being on your hierarchy, your loved one. "Meditate" here means to bring up an image of the being, and use your concentration skills to stay focused on this being. The image will naturally change and flow, but always stay with or return to this being, and avoid images or thoughts which impair lovingkindness. While meditating, actively send feelings of lovingkindness to whomever you are meditating on.

After spending some time meditating on your loved one, move to the next being on your hierarchy. Meditate on this person and send her or him lovingkindness. Continue gradually through your hierarchy. At any one time you might only do one or two items on the hierarchy, or you might do more. But take your time, it is better to go too slow than too fast. Don't move to the next person on your hierarchy until you primarily have loving feelings for the person you are currently working with. And always drop back on the hierarchy when you are beginning again. For example, if one day you stop after number 5 on your hierarchy, then the next time drop back to begin at number 4 or earlier.

While meditating on different people on the hierarchy, always maintain lovingkindness, as through the procedures discussed above relative to generating lovingkindness. In addition, experiment with things you might say to yourself while meditating. Here are some examples from Buddhist lovingkindness meditation: May Connie be free from danger. May Connie be free from mental suffering. May Connie be free from physical suffering. May Connie have ease of well-being. May Connie be happy. May Connie be joyous. May Connie be loving. May Connie be peaceful.

## Group Practice

If it suits you, you can do lovingkindness meditation with a group, but this is not necessary. Instead, you may prefer individual practice using a hierarchy similar to that described for the group. However, if you want to try group practice, here is what to do.

At first all members of the group relax their minds and bodies and generate lovingkindness. Then each person meditates on his or her personal loved one. And then the leader guides the group through a list of beings to meditate on. Everyone is continually sending lovingkindness, and periodically receiving lovingkindness.

Here is one possible list a leader could use: (1) loved one; (2) each person chooses one member of the group (e.g., friend or person nearby); (3) everyone in the group; (4) everyone in the surrounding area (e.g., part of state); (5) everyone in an even larger area (e.g., state); (6) all living beings in this largest area; (7) all living beings in the surrounding area; (8) everyone in the group.

When presenting each item on the list, the leader should use expressions such as those at the end of the last section. For example, "May all living beings in our city be free from physical suffering" and "May everyone in our group have ease of well-being." The leader uses several such expressions for each item on the list and varies the expressions among different items.

At the end of the group meditation everyone sits quietly for a little while basking in lovingkindness. Later in the day, each person reestablishes the feelings of lovingkindness and maintains it as long as possible.

# Awakening

In this section we will consider how the practices you have learned through this manual relate to spiritual and religious practices. This is an optional section of the manual and can easily be skipped by those not interested in these topics. As you know, the practices of this manual are not religious or spiritual in themselves. But because the mental skills you have learned apply to any situation or activity, they must, of course, apply to religious and spiritual practice.

There are many different forces that might motivate a person for spiritual/religious growth, including the following: a quest for happiness or fulfillment that hasn't been satisfied by worldly stuff, a personal crisis, seeking what more there is to life, a quest for peace of mind, a feeling of isolation, a search for meaning, or a desire for a deeper connection and coherence between self and the world. Some people have had experiences which they consider a taste of what lies beyond their small selves, and they wish to explore and learn more. Most people pursue these concerns within the context of their religion, which is great. Some people consider themselves on a spiritual, not religious, path, using the words "spiritual" and "religious" in a variety of different ways. And some people on the journey perceive what they are doing as not being religious or spiritual, perhaps optimizing human potential or uncovering the transpersonal level of being.

There are many ways people think about and describe this journey. Ralph Metzner listed ten common metaphors: awakening from the dream of "reality," uncovering the veils of illusion, moving from captivity to liberation, being purified by inner fire, emerging from darkness to light, progressing from fragmentation to wholeness, journeying to the place of vision and power, returning to the source, dying and being reborn, and unfolding the tree of life. One of these metaphors is not "better" than the others, each person selects or creates the metaphor which is most meaningful or helpful to her or him. For simplicity of this brief discussion, we will use the awakening metaphor. For most people the process of awakening is a gradual process. One wakes up a little, then falls back asleep, then wakes up again, and so on, gradually staying awake longer and not falling so deeply asleep.

The world's great religious and spiritual traditions do not agree at the level of cosmology and philosophy, these usually being dependent on culture. For example, some religions have no gods, some have one God, and some have many gods. In some religions the soul has one human life, followed by some different type of afterlife. In other religions the soul has many human lives. And there are many other points of disagreement. However, at the level of practice—

what you do—there is universal agreement, as discussed below. That is, there is agreement among all the great religions and spiritual traditions about what you do to awaken, how you walk the path, whether you are a Christian, Jew, Muslim, Hindu, Buddhist, Taoist, Native American Indian, or something else. Again, we are talking about practices, not beliefs. Faith, beliefs, and worship are very important to many people and can be very powerful. But these are outside the domain of this manual, and not the focus of the present discussion.

The universal path of awakening consists of ordering one's life along moral and practical guidelines, coupled with the four universal practices of quieting the mind, increasing awareness, opening the heart, and reducing attachments. In Conjunctive Psychology these four practices are called universal somato-psycho-spiritual practices because they dramatically improve the health of body, mind, and spirit.

Ordering one's life along moral and practical guidelines has two components. The first component is seriously adopting a moral code of ethics. The world's religions suggest many things to avoid doing (e.g., killing, stealing, lying, coveting, and inappropriate sexual behavior) and many things to do (e.g., purify body and mind, study spiritual works, and honor parents). Many people will try to be moral because they believe it will affect them in this life and/or a future life. Although moral behavior does have such effects, adepts understand that morality also facilitates awakening, which in most cases is very important.

The second component to ordering one's life along moral and practical guidelines consists of cleaning up biological, psychological, and interpersonal problems. If one wants to awaken, then get free from the drug, stop fighting with the neighbor, get vocational training, or do whatever to make one's life work better. These types of real world problems impair awakening. So warriors and adepts take pleasure at the opportunity to deal with such issues. Some people hope that awakening will free them from the messes in their lives. But this rarely happens, usually awakening just makes one more aware of the mess. On the other hand, you do not have to wait to awaken until all this other work is done; that also won't work and is impractical. So you simultaneously order your life along moral and practical guidelines and employ the four universal practices.

The first practice is quieting the mind. If you don't quiet your mind, all you will know is your own thoughts, usually controlled by the drunken monkey. When you quiet the mind, you open to other types of knowing about yourself and reality, such as the counsel of the Christian Holy Spirit or Buddhist insight knowing. Quieting the mind is emphasized in absorption meditation, Hindu/yogic practices, and mysticism of all Eastern and Western religions. As you know, developing concentration is a powerful way to quiet the mind.

The second practice is increasing awareness, as you have been doing throughout your work with this manual. This includes awareness of body, behaviors, feelings, contents of the mind, processes of the mind, and dynamics of the self. This practice is particularly emphasized in Buddhism under the term "mindfulness."

The third practice is opening the heart, as discussed in the previous sections. This group of practices, coupled with love, devotion, and self-less service, is the heart of Christianity, Mahayana Buddhism, bhakti yoga, and Islamic Sufism.

The fourth practice is reducing attachments, building on what you have learned about attachments in Flexibility III and IV. Reducing attachments is stressed in Western psychology, Buddhism, and Hindu/yogic approaches. Eventually, the self-related attachments become most important for awakening. The adept discovers that his small self that wanted to awaken will never fully awaken. For, to completely awaken involves reducing attachments to and identification with this small self. You are much greater than this!

The best way to awaken is to continually utilize all four practices, perhaps stressing different practices at different times. If you want to decide whether a particular group, workshop, teacher, or book will help your spiritual/religious growth, one question to ask is whether one or more of the four universal practices will be enhanced or impaired.

Awakening does not take you out of the world—it changes your relationship to the world. It is said in many religious traditions that the adept is in the world, but not of it. Awakening allows you to be more fully in the world, with more awareness, clarity, joy, love, freedom, humor, and playfulness. The warrior knows the advantages to being in the world as an optimal situation for awakening. And the adept knows there is nowhere to go, it is a matter of being here now.

## Mental Play

It is good to end the adept level of the manual with play, since it is very important to maintain a playful attitude toward the training in this manual and to life in general. As before, the mental play section is optional, and you should only spend time on the items that are stimulating and/or fun. But everyone should do the last question. Many of the questions have more depth than first appears. Some of the questions are easy, some are hard. Some are superficial, a few are considered by some people to be the most important questions ever asked. But here it is all mental play.

There are no answers for these questions in Appendix III.

1. What would happen if someone went back in time before his birth and stopped his parents from meeting?

2. If there were no time, could one live forever?

3. A theory suggests that the world was created yesterday, with all of its parts of apparent various ages. When the people were created, their minds were filled with memories, as if they had lived before yesterday. How can you prove or disprove this theory?

4. Another theory suggests that time runs backwards from the way it seems. People come into the world old and continually get younger, losing the memories associated with older ages. How can you prove or disprove this theory?

5. Can God learn? If God is omniscient, what is there to learn? If God is omnipotent, why can't God choose to learn?

6. Why is there something, rather than nothing?

7. What would your conscious reality be like if your primary sense mode were smell, rather than vision? Contrast a smell experience with a visual experience of an animal coming into the room you are in and then leaving. When did the animal appear and disappear? What are the implications of your answer?

8. Who would you be if (a) you lived 200 years ago; (b) you were raised in a different country; or (c) you had the same mother but a different father?

9. Discuss the following quote from Shakespeare: "All the world's a stage, and all the men and women merely players." How could this perspective help awakening?

10. Explain the following quote from Satchidananda: "You were perfectly fine until you slowly became de-fined."

11. What are at least two different ways to understand the following quote from Ashok Davar: "Meditation is not what you think"?

12. If you are not your body, feelings, and actions, who are you? If you are not your perceptions, thoughts, and memories, who are you?

13. Since the self, as you observe it, comes and goes, you are not the self. Similarly, the observer or witness comes and goes, so you also are not that. Then who are you?

14. You have actively explored the conscious space between thoughts and between exhalation and inhalation of breathing. What would be the implications if this conscious space was the same identical space for everyone?

15. As an adept level practitioner you have now mastered the basic practices necessary to most effectively use your mind. Of course, there is further you can go with the practices, if you wish. Also, by now you have found the variations of the practices that work best for you and how to best interweave these practices. Knowing all of this, what have you got to add? In your personal supplement to this manual, what would you add that would be useful and important specifically to you? Possibilities include other practices, books, workshops, classes, meditation groups, retreats, therapies, journals, music, and other art. Right now, what is the best thing to say to yourself to motivate and inspire you to be steadfast and carefree on your journey, with this manual and your supplement as two of your guides?

# Level V

# MASTER

The monkey is tamed. The monkey is not injured or dead; in fact the monkey is healthier than ever. Previously the monkey was in charge, but now the monkey serves the master. The monkey is a useful and fun servant.

Periodically, the monkey still runs wild—that's the nature of living. But the master has choice and control. First, the master is immediately aware of when the monkey is drunk or wild. Second, the master has the mental skills to change the monkey's behavior if desired. So the master has choices: Let the monkey run free because it is useful and/or entertaining. Or, redirect the monkey's interest and energy to something else. Or, stop and quiet the monkey.

For example, a memory of some past event starts cycling through the mind. Perhaps the master will let this go. Maybe there is more to be learned by reflecting on this memory. Maybe letting the memory run while observing it from a relaxed position will let some of the associated negative feelings gradually reduce. On the other hand, perhaps the master will choose to stop the memory because there is nothing new to learn or the memory is too negative and harmful. For example, continually dwelling on past mistakes that can't be changed is often an unnecessary cause of stress and suffering. The same choices apply to plans and anticipations of the future. Sometimes this future thinking is helpful in making preparations for a future event, and this should be encouraged. Other times the future thinking is not helpful, and may cause unnecessary worry or concern. In the latter cases the master stops the thoughts.

As a result of mental training, the master lives much more in the here and now than before the monkey was tamed. Previously, an enormous amount of time was spent in the imaginary realms of the dead past and the fantasized future. And much of this time was unproductive or harmful. Now the master chooses how much time to spend in these realms, and thus lives primarily in the here and now. Also, when remembering or anticipating, the master is in the here and now, aware of these mental activities, as opposed to being pulled into and lost in the content of these imaginary realms.

Throughout life the master will always be learning and growing, as well as experiencing the joys and pains of a human existence. The master still suffers, grieves, and ex-periences pain, but these are now much less stressful since the monkey was tamed. More important, the master is now free from the monkey business of self-generated and main-tained sources of suffering. The master has let go of many un-necessary and imagined sources of suffering.

## Awareness V

The master realizes that of all the mental skills, awareness is most important. This is because awareness facilitates every-thing you do! Awareness facilitates interacting with others, playing sports, creating art, praying or meditating, develop-ing concentration, reducing attachments, opening the heart, washing the dog, painting the wall, and everything else. For reasons discussed throughout this manual, awareness im-proves the health of body, mind, and spirit.

Becoming more aware includes becoming aware earlier and earlier in chains of events. Thus, one is aware when one is starting to get anxious or angry, rather than becoming aware after one is caught in the emotion. One is aware when one is starting to crave a piece of chocolate or a cigarette, rather than being aware after it is in one's mouth. This ear-lier awareness makes it much easier for the master to stop unwanted feelings and desires, or at least not act on them. Thus, the master has much more control and choice than before awareness training, which results in the master hav-ing more freedom.

The experiences and the reality in which we live are strongly influenced by our thoughts, feelings, and attitudes. Since the master has developed skills in all these areas, the master can, to a large extent, influence the nature of her or his personal reality.

The degree, breadth, and clarity of the master's awareness fluctuate with different situations and states of the body. But the master is very aware of changes in awareness and has the skills to alter awareness. For example, if a master notices a decrease in clarity of awareness, then concentration and awareness skills are used to bring a clear one-pointed awareness to the object of attention. Or, if a master notices a decrease in breadth of awareness, he or she might consciously look for attachments that are limiting breadth. Cultivating awareness of awareness is an important advanced practice!

## Knowing

There are three different types of knowing: sensory, conceptual, and insight. Sensory knowing is based on the physical senses. If you want to know what a banana tastes like, eat a banana; descriptions from others are not sufficient. Conceptual knowing is based on words, ideas, and concepts, the knowing of philosophy, logic, and mathematics. Conceptual knowing is influenced by reasoning and logical proofs.

Less well known is insight knowing, an immediately experienced intuitive wisdom. Awareness training leads to insight knowing, and this type of knowing is particularly important to the master. For example, one can have conceptual knowledge about one's self, including thoughts, memories, and fantasies. But this is very different than the insight knowing that comes from a direct awareness of the dynamics of one's mind that underlie one's sense of self.

Insight knowing is usually pre-conceptual, it occurs prior to conceptual knowing. When the insight is later thought about, it is translated into conceptual knowing, with the general feeling that the translation is inadequate. For example, a person may have an awakening experience, an insight into the fundamental nature of self and reality. When the person later thinks about or describes the insight, it is felt that the conceptualization of the insight does not contain the power, importance, directness, simplicity, and obviousness of the insight. It is clear that much was lost in the translation.

## Dream Awareness

Working with dreams is an adept and master activity. This includes exploring and analyzing dreams. In addition, occasionally people find that they are briefly aware that they are dreaming. This awareness that one is dreaming is called lucid dreaming. When one is lucid dreaming one can alter the dream in many ways, do things one can't usually do (e.g., fly), and bring in important beings to learn from.

In Tibet, lucid dreaming is the first part of dream yoga. First one learns to bring an awake awareness into the dream state. Then, with this experience as a base, one brings an awake awareness into the non-sleeping state of consciousness. This yoga is thus a practice for personal/spiritual awakening. (Instructions for lucid dreaming are in Appendix VIII, which also includes references for Tibetan dream yoga.)

### Awareness Exercise

During lucid dreaming the master cultivates awareness of the dynamics of the mind that create the dream world. Play with these as a vehicle to better understand them. Cultivate awareness of the nature of one's self in this world and the way it is created by the mind.

With the skills and insights acquired in the dream world, move into the more engrossing world of the non-sleep state of consciousness. Cultivate awareness of the dynamics of the mind that create this world and sense of self.

# Mindfulness

Mindfulness is the central mental training practice of Buddhism. In addition, whereas most of the world's meditation practices emphasize concentration, Buddhism adds meditation that emphasizes awareness via mindfulness. Buddhism's major contribution to world understanding of consciousness, psychology, and spirituality is the understanding of mindfulness: what it is, how to develop it, how it relates to other mental processes, and its results.

So what is mindfulness? At the master level mindfulness is the same as "awareness," as discussed in this manual. Throughout this manual, wherever awareness is discussed, "mindfulness" can be substituted for "awareness." Everything that is said about awareness applies to mindfulness.

Although awareness training can be done by itself, it is usually greatly facilitated by concentration training and cultivating the optimal attitude toward mental training. And all of this training is greatly facilitated by embedding it in breathwork.

## Awareness and Concentration

The behaviors of the mind of awareness and concentration are very distinct processes. They differ in nature, effects, cultivation, and neurological correlates. Discussing/Explaining many of these differences is a critical feature of this book. In Buddhist literature, mindfulness is clearly different than concentration. For example, the Eightfold Path describes eight fundamental aspects of the Buddhist path of living and awakening. Of the eight, number seven is right mindfulness, and number eight is right concentration. (The other six are right understanding, right thought, right speech, right action, right livelihood, and right effort.) The adjective "right" here means perfect, harmonious, in balance, and conscious.

Developing awareness increases concentration, and developing concentration increases awareness. For example, developing concentration quiets the mind and makes it easier to be aware. And developing concentration allows one to stay focused on what one want to be aware of. Conversely, as one develops awareness, one becomes more aware of how concentrated the mind is, which helps in the development of concentration. And as one encourages clarity of awareness, one develops moment-to-moment concentration. In addition, any comprehensive instruction for the cultivation of awareness will include components that develop concentration.

Thus, awareness and concentration are very intertwined, and programs to develop awareness will also develop concentration, intentionally or not. As a result, the term "mindfulness" is often used to mean some combination of awareness training and concentration training. This use of "mindfulness" can be found in some Buddhist scriptures, Western psychology, and many self-help books. Because of this confusion about exactly what the word "mindfulness" means, the term has not been discussed in this manual until now.

It is very important to be very clear about exactly what awareness and concentration are, how they differ, and how they interact. It is easy to lose clarity of perception and understanding if awareness and concentration become blurred together under the guise of mindfulness. Having clear understanding of awareness and concentration is also very important to the master who wishes to help others develop these skills.

## Awareness and Attitude

As has been discussed throughout this book, attitude is important in developing awareness and concentration, opening the heart, and reducing attachments. Thus, developing mindfulness in all of its different meanings is facilitated by acting with intention, having fun, being in the here and now, making friends with oneself, and not-doing. We can add to this list persistent dedication, a welcoming openness to experience, and a readiness to let go.

But attitude is not part of awareness. Attitude affects *developing* awareness, but it is not one of its components. Rather, attitude is something that a person is aware of. Western psychological definitions of "mindfulness" usually include attitude components, such as acceptance or being in the here and now. Including attitude adds further confusion to what mindfulness means, and this often impairs practice and effectiveness.

For example, consider a novice who begins a mindfulness program in which the description of mindfulness includes being in the here and now. To the novice, being in the here and now means being focused on and aware of what is currently happening in the external world, or staying focused on breathing during meditation. But the novice has little control over the drunken monkey and thus has trouble being in the here and now as understood. Hence, the novice feels mindfulness has not been developed at all, but this is all confused! Staying focused involves developing concentration, not awareness. More important, one can be developing awareness even when one is not in the here and now of the external world or one's meditation object.

Developing awareness involves noticing wherever the mind goes and whatever arises in consciousness, regardless of how concentrated the mind is.

## Implications

There are many meditation retreats, therapies, and self help materials that emphasize mindfulness. Some of this is very good, but because of the common confusion about exactly what mindfulness is, many of these programs are far less effective than they could be. Clear understanding of awareness and concentration helps the master choose among the many programs and perhaps improve some of them. Also, for the beginner it is best to learn awareness and concentration from an adept or master, personally or otherwise (e.g., written materials, audio recordings). Because of the great popularity of mindfulness, there are many books and teachers whose knowledge and experienced-based wisdom is far below adept. This often results in mistakes that can mislead the beginner. Some of these mistakes may seem minor or subtle to the less advanced teacher, but they are seen as very important to the master.

# Concentration V

The master has developed concentration to an extent necessary for basic mental control. The master can stay focused at will, such as during reading, listening to music, or fully being with another person. The master has control over thoughts, any thoughts can readily be stopped or redirected. Although

the master periodically uses concentration skills to stay focused on one set of objects, most of the time the master's
concentration is moment-to-moment concentration. That
is, the master has precise focus on whatever arises in consciousness, even as the mind is moving from one object to
another. And the master can quiet and relax the mind, which
relaxes the body. From quieting the mind the master has discovered a peace of mind which is more fulfilling and harmo-
nizing than are sensory pleasures. This peace of mind helps
keep the heart open, makes it easier to accept situations and
people, and allows the body to find its balance and health.

## Awareness Exercise

These awareness practices focus on this stillness or peace of
mind. What is the direct experience of this stillness? What
is the experience of the nature of mind that produces this
stillness? What is the experience of the mind itself within
this stillness?

## Absorption

Periodically people become totally absorbed and lost in what
they are doing. When listening to music a person becomes
totally lost in the music. Or, a musician becomes absorbed
in playing. Whereas before there was a musician playing an
instrument and generating music, now the musician and
instrument are one and music is simply happening. For a
baseball player making the perfect hit of the ball, the bat
may feel like a natural extension of the body. A football or

basketball player suddenly becomes absorbed in a team play that is going as designed, during which time slows down or speeds up. In such cases of absorption the self usually temporarily disappears, as one merges into the activity. And one is usually performing the activity at one's peak capability. Such experiences are sometimes called "peak experiences," being "in the zone" or in "the flow."

These experiences usually just happen when various conditions come together. The people usually did not intentionally cause them and cannot repeat them at will. But the master has the concentration skills to become absorbed at will. Some masters choose to use this skill for advanced meditation practices.

Most of the world's spiritual meditation practices emphasize concentration/absorption. A Christian mystic may meditate on Jesus and lose the self in absorption and surrender. Through absorption a yogi may lose the small self in union with the universal Self, the word *yoga* referring to such a "union." A Sufi poet might be absorbed in the love of God. A spiritual Native American on a vision quest may become one with a spirit animal. In the classic yogic/Buddhist literatures there are described eight levels of absorption, known as *jhanas*.

## Jhanas

The jhanas are a list of eight levels of absorption (*samadhi*) that go past the sensual to form and then past form to the formless. Pursuing the jhanas is not necessary for most people, but it is the path of awakening for many. The jhanas are discussed here as a description of where concentration/absorption can lead and as an example of the meditation practices of some masters. For many reasons people select different objects for concentration and absorption, such as those listed in the previous paragraph. For the master who came the way of this manual, or some equivalent way, the breath is a superior choice of object, at least for the first four jhanas.

While traveling through the jhanas there are a number of experiences and mental states that are commonly encountered. These include rapture, bliss, and equanimity. "Rapture" refers to initial pleasure, excitement, and refreshment, such as when one has found a long sought-after object. Rapture often comes in waves and may be accompanied by phenomena such as flashes of light or hairs rising on the arm. "Bliss" refers to more continuous experiences of joy. And "equanimity" refers to an evenness of mind in which one is not drawn to one mental object more than others. One is equally interested in and attracted to whatever arises in consciousness. It is common to have tastes of some of these three experiences before encountering them in their strongest or purest form. For example, a beginning meditator might experience bits of rapture. And a meditator at the first jhana might get a tasted of equanimity, which is not at its peak until the fourth jhana.

There are two traps to be careful of associated with these experiences. The first trap is becoming attached to an experience, such as bliss. This attachment halts movement through the jhanas, an example of what the Buddha called "stopping within." The second trap is to overestimate one's accomplishments related to the jhanas. One might have a powerful taste of bliss or equanimity and falsely believe one is further along the path of awakening or the journey of the jhanas than one actually is. For both traps the master's previous attachment work is the best prevention.

There is a beautiful logic to the progression through each set of four jhanas. For the first four jhanas this involves the continual quieting of the mind and the increasing of one-pointedness and equanimity. Relatedly, as one progresses through all jhanas, breathing becomes calmer and metabolic functions become more still.

## First Jhana

In this first level of absorption, one can put one's attention on the object of meditation and keep it there for some time. At this jhana there is rapture and bliss. Feelings of biological pain disappear.

## Second Jhana

Through further quieting the mind and increasing one-pointedness, one moves into the second jhana. Here thoughts drop out and there is a singleness of mind. At this jhana there is increased rapture, bliss, and one-pointedness.

## Third Jhana

Movement from the second to the third jhana includes the fading out of rapture, which is much grosser and disturbing than bliss. Equanimity arises and resists the pull of rapture. One still feels bodily pleasure.

## Fourth Jhana

Movement to the fourth jhana involves fading out of bliss, pleasure, and suffering, which are all gross and disturbing relative to the very quiet mind with one-pointed equanimity. There is neither joy nor suffering. One-pointedness and equanimity are now at full strength and clarity, and one is fully in the here and now. This one-pointed equanimity will be maintained through the next jhanas.

Movement into the next four jhanas involves two changes. First is the movement from form to formless, leaving behind all perceptions of form and sense of the body. Second is a switch from emphasizing concentration/absorption to emphasizing contemplation of the object of meditation. The master reflects on the object in an insightful, not conceptual, way.

## Fifth Jhana

Here one extends the meditation object into infinite space, while maintaining awareness of this space about the object. One's consciousness becomes one with this space, which becomes the object of contemplation. There are no perceptions of form within the "consciousness of infinite space."

## Sixth Jhana

Moving from the fifth to the sixth jhana involves switching contemplation from infinite space to the awareness of the space. This contemplation leads to "objectless infinite consciousness."

## Seventh Jhana

The infinite consciousness of the sixth jhana is just one side of the coin. The other side is the non-existence of the infinite consciousness. Switching contemplation to the non-existence leads to awareness of "no-thing-ness." Experiences of the seventh jhana are sometimes discussed in terms like the "void," which can be scary to someone who does not understand this jhana and the need to keep moving.

## Eighth Jhana

Relative to the very quiet mind, any perception is a disruptive disadvantage. So movement to the eighth jhana includes letting go of the perceptions of the sixth and seventh jhanas. For example, when one is in the sixth jhana, there is a subtle perception of infinite consciousness. To move into the eighth jhana one lets go of this perception. However, there is still an ultra-subtle form of "perception" of the eighth jhana. But this is so ultra-subtle that it can't be called perception, and it is thus similar to other mental constituents which are so subtle they can't be said to exist or not exist. Hence the eighth jhana is called "neither perception nor non-perception."

# Awakened Mind

There are many ways to describe the nature of the awakened mind. One Buddhist model which uses concepts in this manual is the seven factors of enlightenment. These seven factors are properties of the awakened mind. They are thus aspects of the mind that are cultivated to improve daily living and facilitate awakening. The seven factors are mindfulness, investigation, effort/energy, rapture/interest, concentration, calm/tranquility, and equanimity.

## Mindfulness

The exact nature of mindfulness has been discussed in a previous section; at the master level it is basically awareness. Mindfulness is the first and primary factor because it awakens and strengthens all the other factors and keeps them in balance. Mindfulness is a purifying force which produces wholesome states of mind. Development of mindfulness is helped by associating with mindful people.

## Investigation

This factor is probing with a silent and peaceful mind. It is not conceptualizing or taking things on faith. It is a matter of seeing for oneself in a way that leads to insight knowing.

## Effort/Energy

This includes the effort to be aware and the effort to awaken. It is a continuation of acting with intention and being a warrior. It includes the understanding that one must do many things by oneself; others can only point the way and provide guidance. This factor also results in a courageous mind that has patience in times of difficulty. Reflecting on the advantages of mental training and/or awakening can motivate right effort.

The more one awakens and the more attachments one reduces, the more energy one has. Also, mindfulness couples with investigation to produce energy.

## Rapture/Interest

This factor is similar to the rapture discussed relative to the jhanas. Included here is profound interest, zestful joy, and welcoming alertness. It results in great delight in exploring truth, free of clinging and grasping.

This factor has a feeling similar to having been in the desert for many days and then coming to a lake. It is accompanied by a lightness of body, mind, and heart.

## Concentration

Concentration has been discussed throughout this manual. For the awakened mind one only needs enough moment-to-moment concentration for clear investigation. The more advanced concentration/absorption of the jhanas is not required, although they are helpful to some people. Concentration provides strength, penetrating power, and peace and stillness. Cultivating optimal concentration requires awareness of concentration.

## Calm/Tranquility

As discussed in this manual, concentration is the primary way to produce a calm mind, which ends agitation and relaxes the body. This calmness improves the clarity of awareness.

Structuring one's environment and lifestyle to be more tranquil facilitates developing this mental factor. Other ways include reducing the following: attachments, lust, and anger.

## Equanimity

Discussed earlier relative to the jhanas, equanimity is an evenness of mind with equal acceptance and receptivity toward all objects of consciousness. A Buddhist analogy is that the sun shines on everything equally. Equanimity purifies awareness, increasing both clarity and breadth. Equanimity balances opposed mental forces, resulting in a state of ease and balance, which then leads to having a balanced attitude toward all living beings and nonliving objects while avoiding attachments.

## Arousal

As mentioned earlier, mindfulness awakens, strengthens, and balances all the other factors. The next three factors all have an arousing effect: investigation, effort/energy, and rapture/interest. The last three factors all have a stabilizing and/or tranquilizing effect: concentration, calm/tranquility, and equanimity. The master is aware of any need for arousing or calming, and then, intentionally or not, brings to bear the appropriate factors.

Note that awakened beings are not necessarily religious and seldom are formal teachers. An awakened person may express the awakened perspective in art, music, dance, poetry, philosophy, mathematics, raking leaves, or cleaning the toilet. And some awakened beings do not conceptually know they are awake, although they have insight knowing about the nature of their being.

## Transpersonal Self

As one progresses through the levels of this manual, there is a significant change in the sense of self. At first this is due to skills acquired by the self and then to the increasing awareness of the self itself. The transpersonal self of the master is very different than the master's earlier novice sense of self.

To understand the transpersonal self, let alone to abide in it, one must understand the relationship between the personal self and the transpersonal self. And to understand the personal self, it is helpful to understand the development of the self in general. Thus, before considering the transpersonal self, we will briefly consider the evolution of the self. Of course, everyone's self journey is unique and not as simple or linear as the following discussion. But the processes of mind and consciousness that underlie the personal and transpersonal selves are universal. And cultivating awareness of these processes is extremely important to the adept and the master.

## Development of Self

When a person is born, there is no sense of self. Then the person gradually develops a distinction between inside and outside the skin. One has more control of things inside the skin, and things that happen to the body feel different than things that happen to objects outside the body. Thus a sense of me vs. not-me evolves, centered on the body. When answering the question "Who am I?" the person would respond "I am this body."

Continually the body learns to do things and the developing sense of self begins to include the body and how it behaves. Now the answer to "Who am I?" is something like "I am a Girl Scout, soccer player, and Kaitlin's best friend."

With more development the body stays related to the self, but now the body is part of the self or something the self inhabits. Similarly, one's behaviors are part of one's self or what the self does. This is the stage of the "personal self," a sense of some self entity that inhabits the body, perceives via the senses, and through acts of will causes some of the behaviors of the body. This personal self has two components: self as object and self as subject. Self as object includes the various thoughts and feelings one has about one's self, plus the image one presents to the world. Self as subject is the sense of some entity that does the perceiving, thinking, and willing. In response to "Who am I?" the answer might be "I am the one answering this question." The novice level personal self can do things to improve life, such as physical conditioning and vocational education. Other areas where things can be done include improving the functioning of the mind with mental training. The possibility and importance of mental training is often overlooked, even though it is usually one of the most important things one can do with one's life. So when the novice discovers mental training, there is usually interest and excitement about the possibilities.

The student level personal self has done enough mental training to see that the practices really work! The student has confidence and trust in this manual and is now motivated and curious to continue training and see where it leads. The self now is acquiring a greater feeling of self-control and mastery, one of the most important factors in the health of body and mind.

The warrior level personal self is far enough along in mental training that the sense of self-control and mastery is very strong. Of course, the warrior is not always successful, but warriors know they have powerful skills that are helpful in many situations. The warrior has experienced so many significant life changes due to mental training that the warrior is very motivated to continue, despite obstacles, attachments, and monkey business.

The adept's awareness training includes being aware of the nature of the personal self. The adept discovers that there is no fixed entity that is this self. Rather, the adept discovers a complex of thoughts, feelings, memories, and attachments that were taken to be the self. Self as object is just mental stuff that can be observed. Self as subject is more subtle and needs to be consciously settled into, rather than just observed. The adept also realizes that the personal self often gets in the way, and one acts more appropriately and spontaneously when this self is not involved. As a result of all this self-related awareness and reflection, the adept becomes less and less identified with the personal self. The question "Who am I?" has now become very profound. "Is the real me the observer of all of this?"

## Transpersonal Level

When the master reflects on "Who am I?" several conclusions are obvious: The master does not identify with the body, although it is a highly valued and respected vehicle. Taking good care of the body and cultivating awareness of the body are very important! The master does not identify with the behaviors of the body or contents of the mind, although these must be worked with. So is the master's sense of self the observer or witness of the body and mind? The observer comes and goes, and thus is not the essence of the master.

What gradually emerges is a transpersonal self outside of time and space, which is prior to and superordinate to the personal self. "Trans" means "beyond," a domain of being that includes the personal and more. The uncovering of the transpersonal self is the essence of awakening. The transpersonal self is always already present; to be realized it simply has to be uncovered. This is done by quieting the mind, increasing awareness, opening the heart, and reducing attachments.

It is commonly believed that to uncover the transpersonal one must somehow suppress, undo, or kill the personal self. This is very wrong! The personal self is a very important functional entity that must be respected, nurtured, and worked with. Awakening consists of disidentifying with the personal self and clearly seeing it for what it is. One lets go of self-related attachments.

Disidentification with the personal self has many powerful effects. One has greater freedom, flexibility, creativity, sanity, and love. One is less vulnerable to things that attack the body or personal self. Contrast this with the teenager who commits suicide when the self-image he created in cyberspace is attacked and humiliated by his peers.

In addition, the mind works better when it isn't involved with unnecessary service to the personal self. For example, when one is identified with the personal self, the mind must spend considerable time and effort continually generating memories and thoughts that create the illusion of a constantly existing personal self. In addition, perceptions and memories have to be altered to better fit the self-image. The master's mind is free from such needs, and thus is more efficient and accurate.

And as the master realizes the transpersonal self, the master recognizes the transpersonal in others. As the master is not the body, behavior, or contents of the mind, so the same is true of all other people. The master values this aspect of every person.

## Helping Others

Recognizing the transpersonal in others greatly facilitates compassion and opening the heart. For beyond the parts that people have in the great play of life, and beyond what one thinks about those parts, there is the profound recognition of the spiritual aspect of everyone. It is realized that everyone is just one of us doing the best he or she can within the part that was given. In addition, to get to the master level, one will have significantly opened the heart, directly and/or indirectly (e.g., as a result of mental training). Thus, the master has great compassion for others and a strong motivation to help them.

Beyond helping the individual, what can we do to help the family, group, country, and world? There are many answers to this, including vocational, social, economic, and political solutions. In addition, helping the individual is often one of the best ways to help the group. As individuals are freed from hunger, anger, anxiety, misperceptions, false assumptions, and attachments, they become more helpful and less problematic to others. Social reform and peace often begin with individual change. Also, the master sees the world as much more interconnected than is usually assumed. Hence, the master realizes how individual change can have very far-reaching effects. Theories of physics, including chaos theory and quantum theory, support this view.

Thus, out of a sense of compassion and service to others and the world, the master is very motivated to help others! One very important way is to help others learn the skills described in this manual. Just about everyone can significantly benefit from some combination of breathwork, concentration, quieting of the mind, awareness training, increased mental flexibility, and reduced attachments.

For masters working in health professions (e.g., nurse, doctor, body worker, yoga instructor, psychologist, spiritual counselor), the application of the basic practices is clear cut. Adding practices such as quieting the mind and increasing awareness to other health practices can significantly improve the overall health benefits, as is shown in considerable impressive research. Many businesses have found that providing workers breaks for meditation and/or yoga improves employees' health, satisfaction, and productivity.

Mental training is also often very helpful in physical activities, such as sports. Developing concentration is very important. Keeping your eye on the ball is critical; a loss of concentration for an instant and a ball is not caught, hit, or kicked. Concentration also helps the player stay focused on the game and not be distracted by crowd noise or the pressure of the moment. Awareness training in sports helps the player be more conscious of where the other players are. For example, when quickly bringing the ball down the court in basketball, it is very important to know where players from both teams are. When a professional basketball team was given awareness training (vipassana), the players reported an increase in awareness of the positions of other players.

When creating a work of art, such as a painting or a piece of music, it is often good to quiet the mind and become totally focused and absorbed in the creation. It is also helpful to get the personal self out of the way and let creativity be more spontaneous. With concentration skills the artist puts aside critical thinking, demands of others, expectations, and other monkey business during the act of creation. Later, one can critically evaluate the work.

There are two issues relative to helping others acquire mental training skills. The first is to recognize that such skills are applicable to a wide range of situations, such as health, sports, and art. The fact that awareness training facilitates anything one does emphasizes its universal applicability. The second issue is how to adapt and specialize the training for different people. How can we take the training practices described in this manual and adapt them to people of different ages, intelligence, interests, needs, and limitations? How can we bring such training into the home, school, and workplace? How can the training be integrated with other activities and services?

Particularly important is to how to help young children begin learning basic mental skills! This can greatly improve their lives and the world. Making such learning simple and fun is usually the best approach. For example, listening to stories or music can be a vehicle to cultivate awareness and/ or concentration.

Parents who meditate, individually or together, often find their young child eventually wants to sit with them and "meditate" too. This can be a time to introduce simple concentration and awareness practices. Children often learn meditation better with guided imagery than with something more difficult and boring, such as watching the breath. Thus, a parent verbally provides the child with a description of changing imagery to focus on.

Jeff Cook is a coach who works with children learning sports, well before some of them later participate in much more competitive versions. His approach to several sports includes the following: The two main objectives are learning the fundamentals of the sport and having fun. Thus, practicing a particular skill may be put into a more playful context. Another basic principle is parity—everyone gets to play and try different positions. Concentration is shaped with verbal cues such as "keep your eye on the ball," "watch the pitcher," "stay in the game," and "cheer on your fellow players." When learning to dribble a basketball, the new player will look down at the dribbling. Awareness is increased by gradually getting the child to look up and about while dribbling. Awareness can be developed in the context of parity, such as everyone touching the basketball or soccer ball before anyone takes a shot. When playing a team that is not as good, the coach can do things to keep from running up the score and simultaneously increase awareness and teach good sportsmanship. For example, the coach tells the best players on the team not to score, but instead work to help weaker players have a chance to score.

Helping others with mental training is a powerful way to reduce suffering and increase health and happiness. There are many drunken monkeys out there that need to be tamed!

## Mental Play

The last two mental play exercises consist of a classic logic paradox and the creation of a personal mandala. The paradox is a wonderful puzzle for reflecting on causality, determinism, and free will, and perhaps cultivating a superordinate understanding of these issues. In the paradox you will have two choices, but people disagree on what choice to make, so it is a good topic for discussion. It is not enough to simply accept the reasons for one of the choices; you must also address the reasons for the other choice.

In creating a personal mandala, you will visually represent many of the things you have been learning about and encountering via this book. At first, most people are hesitant to do this exercise, feeling they are not artistic enough and/or have never done something like this before. In fact, everyone can do this. Most people find it an interesting, fun, and valuable exercise that also results in a powerful object for later reflection and/or meditation.

## Newcomb's Paradox

This puzzle was created by William A. Newcomb, developed and published by Robert Nozich, and popularized by Martin Gardner in his *Scientific American* column. The best discussion is in Gardner's book *Knotted Doughnuts*. The following is a re-telling.

For a few years, a being known as Sal U Kim was a visitor on our planet. Kim studied and mastered human psychology, and then left our planet for good. Many people say Kim is a member of a species far advanced past humans. Some say Kim is an android with a super smart computer brain. And a few think Kim is some type of god. Nobody really knows. We are not even sure what sex or gender Kim is, or if such designations even apply.

What is known is that Kim mastered human psychology and could predict what anyone would do in any situation with an accuracy of 99.99 percent. No matter how complex and difficult the situation, and no matter how much people thought and changed their minds about what to do, Kim could easily and accurately predict what choice they would ultimately make.

Before leaving Earth, Kim left a puzzle specifically for you. On a table in front of you are two closed boxes, A and B. In box A is a thousand dollars. In box B there is either nothing or a million dollars. You now must make one of two choices: You may choose just box B, and thus get nothing or a million dollars. Or, you may choose both box A and box B and thus get $1,000 plus whatever is in box B. Before you immediately take the second choice, there is more to the puzzle.

Before leaving, Kim put $1,000 in box A. Then, if Kim predicted you would choose only box B, Kim put $1,000,000 in box B. But if Kim predicted you would choose both boxes, then Kim put nothing in box B. Kim is now gone and whatever was put in the boxes is still there and won't change. Now, what is your choice?

In favor of taking both boxes is the fact that whatever money is or isn't in box B is not going to change. Simply take both boxes and get $1,000 for sure and maybe also $1,000,000.

In favor of taking just box B is Kim's almost 100 percent accurate ability to predict. Take advantage of this, choose just box B, and get a million. Remember that in making the prediction Kim took into account all your deliberations, changes of mind, and the fact that you know that Kim knows that you know, and so on.

What is your choice and what is wrong in the reasoning for the other choice? Of the people Nozick gave the puzzle to, about half took one choice and half took the other choice.

The following are master level questions: Paradoxes often lead to a new and broader understanding that resolves the paradox and/or explains the different points of view as special cases. Can you provide such an understanding for Newcomb's paradox? For some people it makes a major difference whether Kim's predictions are 100 or 99.99 percent accurate. Why would such a small difference be so important? The paradox involves the personal self making a choice through an act of will. How does this differ for the transpersonal self? Does this resolve the paradox?

## Personal Mandala

The word *mandala* is used in many different ways, from very specific to very general. But here a personal mandala refers to a visual representation of your personal reality. Visual representation may include photographs, pictures, drawings, stickers, and symbols, among many other things. "Your personal reality" means your psycho-spiritual world, which for the mandala could be all psychological, all spiritual, or any combination. Among many other things, your "reality" includes your goals, various roles, forces affecting you, teachers and helpers, and obstacles. What is currently important to you? What is currently happening in your life relative to what is important to you?

Thinking about your life is very important, and making your mandala will stimulate such thinking. But thinking is usually limited in two ways: it is verbal and it is linear. Most thinking is language-based, which means you can only think about things you have words for and reality is distorted to fit the words. But for reflecting or meditating on your life, a picture or a symbol may be more powerful than words, such as in the range or intensity of reactions evoked. So the mandala is built on visual representations rather than words (although some words can certainly be included). For purposes of personal/spiritual growth, the visual is not necessarily better or worse than the verbal—they are both important. Creating a personal mandala is a powerful way to add to the visual.

Verbal thinking is basically linear—you go from A to B to C. Your personal mandala will be more global and holistic. You can see many things at the same time and can better see how disparate components relate and interact with each other. You can see the big picture.

The first step in creating your personal mandala is choice of medium. For many people what works well is a large piece of paper and felt pens, colored pencils, and/or crayons, in a large assortment of colors. You might prefer to play with paint, ceramics, or fabric. You might prefer to create your mandala on canvas, poster board, Styrofoam, or on 3D objects such as a box or ball. Since it is your personal mandala, you can do whatever pleases you and works best for you. Similarly, the following suggestions for constructing a mandala are just possibilities; again, do whatever you want. (To see a collection of very different types of personal mandalas, Google "Mikulas student mandalas" or go to http://uwf.edu/wmikulas/webpage /student_mandalas.htm. Click on a mandala to enlarge.)

Circular mandalas are common and work well. (*Mandala* is a Sanskrit word for "circle.") Draw a large circle that fills most of your paper (or whatever), perhaps using a plate or bowl as a guide. Leave space outside the circle to add things. At the center of the mandala put whatever is at the center of your reality. This center might be a major goal or aspiration, your awakened being or transpersonal self, or a real or symbolic being, such as a Buddha or a Christ.

Next, divide your mandala into about five to ten different sized pie pieces. Each piece is some type of realm of your universe, and its size is proportional to its importance. It might be a realm of one of your roles, personality characteristics, or group of attachments. It might be a realm related to specific people and/or places. Or it might be a realm of particular problems, issues, aspirations, or goals. Consider leaving at least one realm empty at first, to allow for something you later wish to add or to recognize a part of your development or reality currently unknown.

Consider dividing some realms into different parts. This might be done with a line that represents a wall, perhaps with a door in it. There might be a guardian, helper, or demon guarding the door. The different parts of the realm might represent different aspects of the realm or different stages of development within the realm. Some of the dividing lines might be obstacles or barriers to this development.

Now flesh out your mandala with visual representations appropriate to your themes and realms. An emotion or force might be represented by an abstract splash of color. A person or personality trait might be represented by a simple figure. Other possible representations include words, symbols, and pictures. Be creative and free in your choices of visual representation. You can include things such as photos, newspaper clippings, pins, stickers, string, beads, twigs, fabric, glitter, personal objects, or moveable objects.

What you choose to represent might be physical places, forces of nature, emotions, or hindrances. You might include various entities, such as guardian, teacher, trickster, warrior, hero, fool, lover, spouse, muse, creator, mystic, or death. You might include one or more of your personal roles or aspects of your personality, such as child, adult, parent, spouse, lover, protector, manager, critic, power broker, pleaser, expert, artist, intellectual, or mystic.

Outside the circle of the mandala put cosmic forces and/or entities that have a broad influence on your personal reality. Possible entities include teachers, creators, protectors, liberators, and destroyers.

Incorporate concepts, entities, and forces you have learned about using this manual. Possibilities here include the drunken monkey, personal self, concentration, awareness, lovingkindness, components of attitude, factors of enlightenment, and chakras. You can use your mandala to see how all the different things you learned in this book fit together and influence each other. Doing so will help you fine-tune your practice.

Meditate on your mandala during construction. Consider giving a "voice" to different parts of the mandala, so they can talk to you and to each other. Carefully listen to their conversations.

When the mandala is finished, periodically use it as an object of meditation. Let this be a time of integration, including the synthesis of things learned with this manual.

## Farewell

Congratulations! By using the practices of this book, you have done one of the most significant things you can do with your life, but of course, you know this now. Your whole life is much better than it was, and probably much better than you imagined it could be. You also have probably introduced some of the practices to people important to you, perhaps greatly improving their lives as well. Maybe you have given them a copy of this book.

Let us review a few of the things you have learned: You can now control your thoughts and emotions. You can relax your mind and body at will and reduce or eliminate stress. You can keep your mind focused on what you want and resist distractions. Your perception and thinking is much clearer and sharper. You are now much more aware of your body, feelings, and mind, as well as of other people and the environment. Your increased awareness improves everything you do and reduces accidents and mistakes. Your mind is much more flexible and creative, and you have learned how to free yourself from limiting assumptions and attachments. You know the power of breathwork to improve health, relax body and mind, and re-center yourself in the here and now. You realize there is much more to the attitudes of living than you probably expected, and are impressed by the subtlety and power of attitudes. And you know that the process of awakening is a natural and attainable level of development for everyone—some would say it is the purpose of living.

I wish you well and know you will contribute to bringing our world more health, happiness, fulfillment, harmony, and peace.

# *Resources*

## Overview

The first book below is a readable college textbook with elaboration and discussion of topics of this book, plus comprehensive references. The second book is a useful companion to *Taming the Drunken Monkey*, providing practical behavior strategies for many common problems of living. *Skills of Living* can be accessed for free online (Google "Mikulas Skills of Living," or go to uwf.edu/wmikulas/books).

Mikulas, William. L. *The Integrative Helper: Convergence of Eastern and Western Traditions.* Wadsworth, 2002.

————. *Skills of Living: A Complete Course in You and What You Can Do About Yourself.* University Press of America, 1983.

# Level I: Novice

## Breathwork

Farhi, Donna. *The Breathing Book.* Owl Books, 1996.

Lewis, Dennis. *Free Your Breath, Free Your Life.* Shambhala, 2004.

## Relaxation

*New Directions* and *Relaxation Dynamics* cover muscle relaxation, and the latter also includes other ways to relax.

Bernstein, Douglas A., Thomas D. Borkovec, and Holly Hazlett-Stevens. *New Directions in Progressive Relaxation Training.* Praeger, 2000.

Maxmen, Jerrold S. *A Good Night's Sleep.* Warner, 1981.

Morin, Charles M. *Relief from Insomnia.* Doubleday, 1996.

Smith, Jonathan C. *Relaxation Dynamics.* Research Press, 1985.

## Mental Flexibility

De Bono, Edward. *De Bono's Thinking Course.* Barnes & Noble, 1994.

————. *Lateral Thinking.* Harper Colophon, 1973.

Gardner, Martin. *Aha!* W. H. Freeman, 1978.

Sloane, Paul, Des MacHale, and Michael A. DeSpezio. *The Ultimate Lateral & Critical Thinking Puzzle Book: Master Your "Thinking-Outside-the-Box" Skills.* Sterling, 2002.

# Level II: Student

## Creativity

Adams, James L. *Conceptual Blockbusting: A Guide to Better Ideas,* third ed. Basic Books, 1990.

Ayan, Jordan. *Aha!* Crown, 1997.

Von Oech, Roger. *A Whack on the Side of the Head,* rev. ed. Warner, 1998.

Wujec, Tom. *Five Star Mind: Games & Puzzles to Stimulate Your Creativity & Imagination.* Doubleday, 1995.

## Mental Play

Martin Gardner has many excellent books of collections of logic puzzles, games, mathematical recreations, and related philosophy and mental amusement. Raymond Smullyan has a number of books of logic puzzles of the truth-tellers and liars variety, such as logic puzzle 16. The first book is a collection of a unique type of logical chess problem and the second of his two books below is a collection of logic puzzles.

Dudeney, Henry E. *536 Puzzles & Curious Problems.* Scribner, 1967.

Fixx, James F. *Solve It!* Doubleday, 1978.

Fujimura, Kobon. *The Tokyo Puzzles.* Scribner, 1978.

Gardner, Martin. *Entertaining Mathematical Puzzles.* Dover, 1961.

Mott-Smith, Geoffrey. *Mathematical Puzzles.* Dover, 1954.

Smullyan, Raymond. *The Chess Mysteries of Sherlock Holmes.* Knopf, 1979.

———. *What Is the Name of This Book?: The Riddle of Dracula and Other Logical Puzzles.* Prentice Hall, 1978.

# Level III: Warrior

## Awareness and Pain

Kabat-Zinn, Jon. *Full Catastrophe Living: Using the Wisdom of Your Body and Mind to Face Stress, Pain, and Illness.* Delta, 1990.

## Attitude

Easwaren, Eknath. *Take Your Time: Finding Balance in a Hurried World.* Nilgiri Press, 1994.

## Pranayama

Iyengar, B. K. S. *Light on Pranayama.* Crossroad, 1987.

Rosen, Richard. *The Yoga of Breath.* Shambhala, 2002.

Swami Rama. *Path of Fire and Light.* Himalayan Publishers, 1986.

Swami Rama, Rudolph Ballentine, and Alan Hymes. *Science of Breath,* rev. ed. Himalayan Publishers, 1998.

## *Attachments*

Allenbaugh, Eric. *Wake-up Calls.* Fireside, 1992.

Goleman, Daniel. *Vital Lies, Simple Truths: The Psychology of Self-Deception.* Simon & Schuster, 1988.

Keyes Jr., Ken. *Handbook to Higher Consciousness,* fifth ed. Living Love Center, 1975.

Maul, Gail, and Terry Maul. *Beyond Limit: Ways to Growth and Freedom.* Scott, Foresman, 1983.

## *Meditation*

Bodian, Stephen. *Meditation for Dummies,* second ed. ADG Books, 2006.

Fontana, David. *The Meditator's Handbook: A Comprehensive Guide to Eastern & Western Meditation Techniques.* Element, 1992.

Goleman, Daniel. *The Meditative Mind.* Tarcher, 1988.

McDonald, Kathleen. *How to Meditate: A Practical Guide,* second ed. Wisdom, 2005.

Murphy, Michael, Steven Donovan, and Eugene Taylor. *The Physical and Psychological Effects of Meditation: A Review of Contemporary Research With a Comprehensive Bibliography, 1931–1996.* Institute of Noetic Sciences, 1997.

Suzuki, Shunryu. *Zen Mind, Beginner's Mind.* Weatherhill, 1970.

## Vipassana

Goldstein, Joseph. *Insight Meditation: The Practice of Freedom.* Shambhala, 1993.

Mahasi Sayadaw. *Practical Insight Meditation* and *The Progress of Insight.* (Author's note: Begin with *Practical Insight.*) Buddhist Publication Society, 1980, 1978.

Pandita, U. *In This Very Life: The Liberation Teachings of the Buddha.* Wisdom, 1992.

Rosenberg, Larry. *Breath by Breath: The Liberating Practice of Insight Meditation.* Shambhala, 1999.

Silananda, U. *The Four Foundations of Mindfulness.* Wisdom, 1990.

## Games

Angiolino, Andrea. *Super Sharp Paper & Pencil Games.* Sterling, 1995.

Brandreth, Gyles. *The World's Best Indoor Games.* Pantheon, 1981.

Parlett, David. *The Penguin Book of Word Games.* Penguin, 1982.

Pritchard, David B. *Brain Games: The World's Best Games for Two.* Penguin, 1982.

Schmittberger, R. Wayne. *New Rules for Classic Games.* Wiley, 1992.

## Go

Haruyama, Isamu, and Yoshiaki Nagahara. *Basic Techniques of Go,* third ed. Ishi Press, 1992.

Ishida, Akira, and James Davies. *Attack and Defense.* Ishi Press, 1980.

Iwamoto, Kaoru. *Go for Beginners.* Pantheon, 1972.

Kosugi, Kiyoshi, and James Davies. *38 Basic Joseki.* Ishi Press, 1973.

Nagahara, Yoshiaki. *Strategic Concepts of Go.* Ishi Press, 1972.

## Bridge

*Bridge for Dummies* and *The Joy of Bridge* are for beginners; *New Approach, Countdown,* and *Watson's* are for intermediate players; *Complete BOLS Bridge* and *Master Play* are for advanced players. Many good bridge writers have each written several good books, including authors Eddie Kantar, H. W. Kelsey, Mike Lawrence, Victor Mollo, and Terence Reese.

Brock, Sally, ed. *The Complete Book of BOLS Bridge Tips.* Chess & Bridge LTD, 1997.

Grant, Audrey, and Eric Rodwell. *The Joy of Bridge.* Fireside, 1984.

Kantar, Eddie. *Bridge for Dummies,* third ed. IDG Books, 2012.

———. *A New Approach to Play and Defense.* HDL Publishing, 1986.

Kelsey, Hugh W. *Countdown to Better Bridge.* Devyn Press, 1986.

Reese, Terrence. *Master Play.* Cornerstone, 1960.

Watson, Louis H. *Watson's Classic Book on the Play of the Hand at Bridge,* enlarged ed. Barnes and Noble, 1958.

# Level IV: Adept

## Self as Subject

Adyashanti. *True Meditation: Discover the Freedom of Pure Awareness.* Sounds True, 2006.

Godman, David, ed. *Be As You Are: The Teachings of Sri Ramana Maharshi.* Arkana, 1985.

Klein, Jean. *Transmission of the Flame.* Third Millennium Publications, 1990.

## Opening the Heart

Armstrong, Karen. *Twelve Steps to a Compassionate Life.* Anchor Books, 2010.

Hendricks, Gay. *Learning to Love Yourself.* Spectrum, 1982.

Hopkins, Jeffrey. *Cultivating Compassion: A Buddhist Perspective.* Broadway Books, 2001.

Salzberg, Sharon. *Lovingkindness.* Shambhala, 1997.

Simon, Sidney B., and Suzanne Simon. *Forgiveness.* Warner, 1990.

## Awakening Practices

Mikulas, William L. *The Way Beyond: An Overview of Spiritual Practices.* Theosophical Publishing House, 1987. (This book can be accessed for free online. Google "Mikulas the Way Beyond" or go to uwf.edu /wmikulas/books).

Walsh, Roger. *Essential Spirituality: The 7 Central Practices to Awaken Heart and Mind.* Wiley, 1999.

## Mental Play

Falletta, Nicholas. *The Paradoxicon: A Collection of Contradictory Challenges, Problematic Puzzles, and Impossible Illustrations.* Doubleday, 1983.

Lightman, Alan. *Einstein's Dreams.* Warner, 1994. (Stories about different types of time.)

Rucker, Rudolf. *The Fourth Dimension: A Guided Tour of Higher Universes.* Houghton Mifflin, 1984.

Smullyan, Raymond. *5000 B.C. and Other Philosophical Fantasies: Puzzles and Paradoxes, Riddles and Reasonings.* St Martin's Press, 1983.

# Level V: Master

## Jhanas

Brahm, Ajahn. *Mindfulness, Bliss, and Beyond: A Meditator's Handbook.* Wisdom, 2006.

Khema, Ayya. *Who is My Self?: A Guide to Buddhist Meditation.* Wisdom, 1997.

## Awakened Mind

Hixon, Lex. *Coming Home: The Experience of Enlightenment in Sacred Traditions.* Tarcher, 1978.

Mitchell, Stephen, ed. *The Enlightened Mind: An Anthology of Sacred Prose.* HarperPerennial, 1991.

Stace, Walter T. *The Teaching of the Mystics.* Mentor, 1960.

White, John, ed. *What is Enlightenment?* Paragon House, 1985.

## Inspirational Reading

Barks translates the poetry of the heart of Rumi, Islam's foremost mystical poet. Drawing from traditions around the world, Feldman and Kornfield provide stories and Huxley gives us a classic anthology. Klein speaks from the viewpoint of *advaita*, the nondual form of *vedanta*, the precursor of yoga/Hinduism. Kornfield provides many stories and lessons of awakening, including what happens after enlightenment experiences. And Ram Dass and Gorman present stories and discussion of issues of personal/spiritual growth for people in the helping professions.

Barks, Coleman, trans. *The Essential Rumi.* Castle Books, 1995.

Feldman, Christina, and Jack Kornfield, eds. *Stories of the Spirit, Stories of the Heart: Parables of the Spiritual Path from Around the World.* HarperCollins, 1991.

Huxley, Aldous. *The Perennial Philosophy: An Interpretation of the Great Mystics, East and West.* Harper & Row, 1941.

Klein, Jean. *Transmission of the Flame.* Third Millennium Publications, 1990.

Kornfield, Jack. *After the Ecstasy, the Laundry: How the Heart Grows Wise on the Spiritual Path.* Bantam Books, 2000.

Ram Dass and Paul Gorman. *How Can I Help?* Knopf, 1985.

# *Appendix I:*
# *Awareness Questionnaire*

**Instructions:** On the line before each statement put a number from 1 to 5, using the following code to indicate how often the statement is true for you. Put an NA (not applicable) on the line if the statement doesn't apply to you. Put an X if the statement is unclear.

Do not write your answers in this book. Either write your answers on a separate piece of paper or photocopy the questionnaire and write on the copy. The reason for this is that you will want to use the questionnaire repeatedly over time, and you don't want to be influenced by previous answers. Be sure to put the date on the answers each time.

Do not combine or add up your answers in any way. What is important is your answer to each individual item.

Think about each item to help you identify areas for special attention in awareness training. Similarly, when you answer the questionnaire again, compare each item's answer with your previous answer to the same item. This will help you see where you are improving and where you need to put more emphasis.

5 = always or very often true of me

4 = often true of me

3 = occasionally true of me

2 = seldom true of me

1 = never or almost never true of me

NA = does not apply to me

X = the meaning of the statement is unclear

____ I get anxious or angry before I realize why.

____ When listening to people, I miss part of what they say because I am thinking about what they said, what I will say, or other things.

____ After leaving home I wonder about something I may have forgotten to do, such as turning off the coffee pot, closing the windows, or locking the door.

____ When I am in a particular mood, my mind contains related music or images.

____ If I put my attention on a physical pain, the pain will increase or decrease.

____ When I am sitting down, I am aware of the sensations of sitting.

____When I am influenced by desire or anger, I observe how it affects my mind.

____ I notice a difference between sounds and the hearing of the sounds.

____ I lose track of time.

____ I unconsciously move my body when it is un- comfortable without noticing the discomfort.

____ Before becoming anxious I notice thoughts and feelings that lead to the anxiety.

____ I eat much of a meal without really noticing the tastes.

____ I experience muscle tension I do not see coming on.

____ I get depressed without knowing why.

____ I notice how my beliefs often influence what I see and how I feel.

____ When I am thinking, I am aware of the thoughts and the fact that I am thinking.

____ I don't pay attention to my breathing, such as whether it is shallow or deep.

____ I forget where I have left things, such as my glasses or where I parked the car.

____ I notice sensations of pleasure or pain before I label them.

____ I notice how thoughts and feelings gradually arise in my consciousness.

____ I know the difference between eating when I am hungry and eating for other reasons.

____ I am aware of when I am seeking sensual pleasure.

____ I catch myself viewing other people in terms of stereotypes or preconceptions.

____ I will say or do something without actually intending to do it.

____ I know when I am in a situation that will lead to my being angry.

____ I am aware of my body positions when talking with others.

\_\_\_\_ I notice how much I am involved in what is currently happening or how much I am lost in thought and fantasy.

\_\_\_\_ By the end of the day I don't remember some of the snacks I have eaten.

\_\_\_\_ I am basically aware of how distracted or focused my mind is.

\_\_\_\_ I get severe headaches before noticing them coming on.

\_\_\_\_ I am aware of the effects on my mind when I feel worry, uncertainty, or ill-will.

\_\_\_\_ I suddenly find myself eating or drinking something or lighting up a cigarette without having given any thought to doing it.

\_\_\_\_ I feel there is a part of me that just watches my life.

\_\_\_\_ When listening to music I enjoy, my mind runs off in directions other than music.

\_\_\_\_ I get particularly happy and cheerful without knowing just why.

\_\_\_\_ I lose track of money I spend.

____ I don't respond so much to what I perceive, but more to how I label or categorize what I perceive.

____ I notice how feelings, sensations, and thoughts gradually weaken and leave my consciousness.

____ I know when it is inevitable that I will become angry or anxious before I actually feel the emotion.

____ Part of my mind is filled with thoughts, visual images, and/or music.

____ I miss appointments because I have gotten lost in other activities.

____ I notice the effects on my body and mind of what I have eaten or drunk.

____ When I am looking at something, I am aware of what I see and the process of seeing itself.

____ I am aware of an intent to do something before I actually do it.

____ I feel that I am an observer watching my mind.

*Appendix II:*

# *Muscle Relaxation*

Relaxing your muscles is one of the most effective ways to relax your body. And relaxing your body helps to relax your mind. Here you will learn a set of exercises to relax your muscles. At first it will take some time to do these exercises, about a half-hour per day. But after a couple of weeks you can do them in much less time, and then eventually you can relax just by willing it. Everyone can benefit from doing these exercises for a few weeks, even if now or later you have another way to relax. These exercises will put you more in touch with your body and also give you a sense of what a relaxed body can or should feel like.

The exercises are usually best done in a lounge chair with your feet on the floor. However, they can be done in other positions such as lying on the floor. It is usually not good to do them lying in bed since you will have a tendency to fall asleep. Do the exercises at least once a day, twice a day if possible. Take your time when doing the exercises. For many people it takes 30 to 45 minutes at this stage. In these exercises first you will tense a muscle for 5 to 10 seconds and then relax the muscle for 20 to 30 seconds, releasing the tension as fast as possible. When tensing the muscle you should focus your attention on the feelings of tension. Feel the tension! When relaxing the muscle you should focus your attention on the change from tension to relaxation. Feel the tension flow out of the muscle. Feel the change from tension to relaxation. Feel the relaxation in the muscle.

Below is a list muscles to go through with this procedure. Use this list for a while, as it has been well tested. If you have any special physical limitations, such as a trick knee or spinal injury, be sure to check with your doctor before doing any of these exercises. If you have certain muscles that tend to get cramps, do not tense them as hard as other muscles. Feel free to spend extra time with those muscles of particular interest to you. For example, if you get tension headaches, spend some extra time with the muscles of the shoulders and neck. As you do these exercises you will become more and more aware of your body and the muscles you wish to work with. For example, you may find out over time that as you worry you tense muscles in your stomach or jaw or forehead. Then you would want to do extra work with these muscles. Eventually, you may even devise whole sets of special exercises for yourself.

Sometimes when you relax your body you may experience unusual body feelings such as muscle twitches or the sensation of floating. These are common and nothing to worry about. Just let the feelings go, notice them, and continue to relax. Remember in doing these exercises that you are always in control! For a few people, doing these exercises makes them more aroused rather than more relaxed. If this happens to you, decrease how hard you tense the muscles. Gradually and slowly tense until you feel the slightest increase in tension, then stop tensing.

Now it is time to actually do the exercises. Close your eyes and do some deep breathing. Then begin muscle relaxation using the muscle list below. Keep your eyes closed as much as possible. Go through the list one muscle group at a time, tensing very hard the muscles as described. (Alternative ways of tensing some of the muscles are given in parentheses. You may wish to try these alternatives later on.) Tense and relax each muscle group twice in a row, tensing and relaxing as described above with your attention on the feelings of tension and relaxation. Each time after you have tensed and relaxed a muscle group twice, relax and give yourself suggestions to feel "heavy, calm, and relaxed." Then move on to the next muscle groups on the list. Each time you see "deep breathing" on the list, spend a couple of minutes doing deep breathing. Let yourself relax even more with each outbreath. Let each outbreath say "relax" to you.

When you complete the list stay quiet and relaxed with your eyes closed. Then slowly count yourself down from 1 to 5, letting yourself relax even more with each count. Then stay relaxed for a few minutes. After this, slowly count yourself back from 5 to 1 and slowly open your eyes. Get up slowly and pay attention to all your feelings. Remember, you are always in control.

You may find it useful to make an audio recording of you or someone else giving you all the above instructions to tense and to relax, which muscles to tense, and when to do deep breathing. This allows you to put full attention on your feelings without thinking about what to do next. However, the counting from 1 to 5 and back to 1 you should always do yourself.

## Muscle Relaxation List

The following is the list of muscle groups to be tensed and relaxed. For most people tensing and relaxing each of the following twice in a row works best. Alternative ways of tensing are in parentheses.

- **right hand:** make a fist (bend hand back at wrist)

- **right biceps:** bend elbow and "make a muscle" tightening the large muscle in the upper part of the arm (press elbow against arm of chair)

- **right arm:** push arm straight out in front with fingers spread (reach for sky, or out to side, or back over head, or one after the other)

- **left hand:** make a fist (bend hand back at wrist)
- **left biceps:** bend elbow and "make a muscle" tightening the large muscle in the upper part of the arm (press elbow against arm of chair)
- **left arm:** push arm straight out in front with fingers spread (reach for sky, or out to side, or back over head, or one after the other)
- **deep breathing:** take several deep breaths focusing on your diaphragm or the breath at the tip of your nose
- **forehead:** wrinkle forehead and raise eyebrows (lower eyebrows and make exaggerated frown)
- **eyes:** close tight and wrinkle nose (open eyes as wide as possible)
- **mouth:** pucker lips and then frown, push tongue against roof of mouth (open mouth as wide as possible or grin broadly)
- **jaws:** bite teeth together and pull back corners of mouth
- **neck:** rotate head in both directions rolling the neck (push chin against chest or head against back of chair)
- **deep breathing:** take several deep breaths focusing on your diaphragm or the breath at the tip of your nose

- **shoulders:** push shoulder blades back as if to touch, then shrug shoulders and pull head, lowering chin to chest

- **back:** arch lower back sticking out chest and stomach

- **chest:** take a deep breath, force out chest, hold breath

- **stomach:** tighten stomach muscles (pull stomach in and/or push stomach out)

- **deep breathing:** take several deep breaths focusing on your diaphragm or the breath at the tip of your nose

- **legs:** (a) push against the floor, first heels and then toes; or (b) with legs straight out, first flex your feet, pulling toes toward you, and then extend, pushing toes away from you while turning the feet inward and curling the toes

- **deep breathing:** take several deep breaths focusing on your diaphragm or the breath at the tip of your nose

- **1 to 5 count:** to go deeper into relaxation

- **5 to 1 count:** to bring you back

## Muscle Relaxation Practice

You should do the previous exercises for about two to three weeks. Then you can start to shorten the exercises by combining muscle groups and tensing several groups at once:

- both hands and arms together

- forehead, eyes, mouth, jaws, and neck together

- shoulders, back, chest, and stomach together

- legs

Here you will need to develop your own best way of combining the muscle groups for tensing, the way that suits your needs and interests. With the exception of combining muscle groups, the rest of the practice should be the same, including keeping your attention on the tension and relaxation and the use of deep breathing.

After you have done the above exercises with combined muscle groups for at least two to three weeks, you can move to the next stage. Here you should practice going through the list of muscles and relax them, but without tensing them first. That is, you do everything the same as at the beginning of these exercises but leave out the tensing. Be sure to include giving yourself relaxation suggestions such as "calm and relaxed" while relaxing the muscles. Then every couple of days do the exercises with tensing. Continue to practice this until you can relax your muscles at will.

Finally, practice relaxing combinations of muscles without tensing them. Then move toward relaxing your whole body at one time.

Some people find that it helps their relaxation if they add the imagining of a relaxing scene. The imagined scene might be sitting on a sofa in front of a fire on a cold winter night, lying on soft grass on a warm spring day and looking at the clouds float by, lying on the beach on a warm summer day, or lying in a tent listening to a light rain.

## *Appendix III:*
## *Mental Play Answers*

## Lateral Thinking

5.  Stand back to back.

6.  Stand on two sides of a closed door with the newspaper under the door.

7.  If a square manhole cover is tipped on edge, it can fall through the hole diagonally.

8.  The oil for packing the fish is more expensive per volume than the fish.

9.  Throw the ball straight up in the air.

10. Have each driver drive another's car. The prize is for the car that comes in last, not the driver.

11. Deal the bottom card to yourself and then continue dealing from the bottom counterclockwise, assuming you were originally dealing clockwise and to yourself last in rotation.

12. Flip the first switch and leave it on for a few minutes. Then switch it off, flip the second switch on, and hurry and open the closet door. If the light bulb is on, it is switch two. If the bulb is off but feels warm, it is switch one. Otherwise it is switch three.

13. Add another A pill. Cut all four pills in half, separating tops and bottoms. Take the tops today and bottoms tomorrow.

# Logic I

14. Notebook = $1.05; Pencil = 5 cents.

15. Three. At this point you must have a pair of one color or the other.

16. Neither a knight nor a knave can say "I am a knave." For a knight it would be lying and for a knave it would be telling the truth. Hence B is lying and is a knave, and C is telling the truth and is a knight.

17. They are the same. Since the two glasses contain equal amounts of liquid at the beginning and the end, the amount of wine in the water equals the water no longer in the water glass equals the amount of water in the wine.

## Assumptions

18. They did not play each other.

19. The other end of the rope is not attached to anything.

20. The room did not get dark because it was daytime.

21. The bird was deaf.

22. The girls are two of triplets.

23. The surgeon was Arthur's mother.

24. Tom was a horse.

25. The tire tracks are from a wheelchair and Jay is the only one sitting in a wheelchair, which also has mud on its tires.

26. You need 2000 (two thousand) pennies to have $20.00.

27. Two. The boat and ladder rise and fall with the tide.

28. 1½ inches. The bookworm travels through the pages of the second volume only. Visualize the books on a shelf and exactly where the bookworm starts and stops.

# Logic II

29. The bear is white. The last lap of his tour is at right angles to the first leg. If the bear is headed south on reaching his den, and left it in a due south line, his den must be on the North Pole, from which every direction is due south. Hence he is a polar bear.

30. Your circle is black too. Assume you have a red circle. Then friend A will see a red circle and a black circle. A will figure out he or she must have a black circle, otherwise friend B would not be raising a hand. Similarly, friend B could use the same reasoning to determine she or he has a black circle. Since neither of your friends figured out the color, your circle is probably also black.

31. Before leaving home she puts a new battery in her clock and notes the time it shows. At her friend's she notes the "real" time she arrives and leaves. At home she tells from her clock how long she had been away. Subtracting from this the time she had spent at her friend's, she knows how long she had walked back and forth. Adding half of this to the time she left her friend's house gives her what time it is now.

32. White. With each drawing out of two marbles and putting one back, the number of white marbles in the bag stays the same or is reduced by two. Hence, since you began with an odd number of white marbles, there must always be an odd number. So if there is one marble, it must be white.

## Appendix IV:
## *Learning and Studying*

In this section you will learn strategies to improve your studying and better remember what you've studied. You have learned the importance of setting for your way of practice. The same logic applies to studying, although the setting for studying should be different than the setting for your way of practice. Ideally, you would have a chair and table that you only use for studying and related work. If you use the same chair for studying, watching television, talking on the phone, checking Internet sites, and daydreaming, then that chair has many associations that interfere with good studying. It is better if the only thing you do in that chair is focus on your studies. You also want your study area free of distractions like photos, cell phones, and music that engages you. If it is not practical to have a separate chair and space for studying, then perhaps you can re-arrange things to create a study space when needed, or drape the chair with a certain cover used only when you study. You also want to have good lighting and fresh air.

The concentration you are developing will be a very powerful aid in studying. Being able to keep your mind more focused on what you are studying will improve your learning and memory, and will decrease the amount of time needed to study. Here is how it works: If your mind leaves what you are studying, gently and firmly bring it back. If the monkey is particularly wild, leave the study area, relax, and then return. Break up your study time into units that correspond with approximately how long you can stay at least moderately focused on the material. For one of the topics you study, for example, it may be that fifteen minutes is about how long you can stay focused. Then you take a short break, relax, and return for the next fifteen-minute session. With concentration development, you will increase the amount of time you can stay concentrated while studying.

Learning and memory are best when you space the learning out over time, rather than mass it together. Thus, learning is easier and memory is better when you study something for a half an hour a day, four days a week, for two weeks, than if all the studying is crammed into one evening. Cramming is a very common mistake among college students who often wait until the day before an exam to really start studying.

To motivate yourself to study more frequently, look for ways to reward yourself for studying. Look for things that you like to do, such as communicating with friends, watching a video, listening to music, taking a shower, baking cookies, or playing a game. Then require yourself to do a certain amount of studying before you reward yourself with doing the pleasant activity.

When studying, do not just passively read what you want to learn. Rather, get actively involved in thinking about what you are learning. Ask yourself questions about what you are learning and compare it with other things you have learned. If you are going to be tested on what you learned, ask yourself questions you might encounter in the testing. If it is going to be an essay exam, ask yourself and answer essay-type questions. If it is going to be a multiple-choice exam, make up multiple-choice questions for yourself. If it will be an oral exam, practice formulating your ideas to possible questions, and rehearse summarizing your answers out loud. Practice what you will be required to do.

A well-known study system developed by Francis Robinson is the SQ3R method, which stands for "Survey, Question, Read, Recite, and Review." There are now many variations of this system, including the SQ4R method. The steps in this system are Survey, Question, Read, Reflect, Recite, and Review. During Survey you quickly preview the material to get an overview of the content and organization, paying attention to headings and subheadings. During Question you ask yourself questions about what you overviewed, keying off of the headings with questions beginning with who, what, where, and why. During Read you read through the material and try to answer your questions. During Reflect you think about what you read, how the different parts relate to each other, and how it all relates to other things you know. During Recite you practice remembering main points and questions, with reciting out loud working well for many people. Finally, during Review you go back and actively review the material. After you are familiar and comfortable with a system such as SQ4R, you can devise your own system that works best for you.

To help make meaningful sense of what you are studying, try the TCDR strategy, developed by Tim Walter, Glen Knudsvig, and Donald Smith. TCDR stands for "Topic, Class, Description, and Relevance." For Topic you identify the key topics that you must understand. Then for Class you identify what is the class to which a topic belongs. That is, what is the whole of which the topic is a part? For example, the topic "hammer" is a part of the class "tools." Next you consider a Description of the topic, including such things as characteristics, features, properties, and appearance. Finally, you think about the topic's Relevance, including use and importance.

Using some of the above strategies, you can learn more effectively in less time and better remember what you learned. Your concentration skills will be particularly useful here.

Your flexibility skills will be helpful in taking exams. Finally, as part of your awareness training, you want to try to be aware of all components of studying, including how the setting affects you, how motivated you are, how concentrated your mind is, and how you think when studying.

## Resources

Dembo, Myron H. *Motivation and Learning Strategies for College Success: A Self-Management Approach.* Erlbaum, 2000.

Morgan, Clifford Thomas, and James Deese. *How to study,* second ed. McGraw-Hill, 1969.

Walter, Timothy L., and Al Siebert. *Student Success: How to Succeed in College and Still Have Time for Your Friends,* eighth ed. Harcourt Brace Jovanovich, 2000.

Walter, Timothy L., Glenn M. Knudsvig, and Donald E. P. Smith. *Critical Thinking,* second ed. Wadsworth, 2003.

# *Appendix V:*
# *Concentration Game*

Thoroughly shuffle a full deck of fifty-two cards. Place the cards individually face down in rows of some type. The first player turns over any two cards for everyone to see. If they happen to match in value, such as two fives or two jacks, the player keeps them. The player keeps turning over sets of two and keeps matching pairs until he turns over two that don't match. When they don't match, the cards are returned face down to their original place, and it is now the next player's turn. The game continues until all pairs of cards have been taken up. The player with the most cards wins. The game is best with two players, but can be played with more.

# *Appendix VI:*
# *Bulls and Cows Game*

1. The code-maker writes down a sequence of four letters, where each letter can be one of the six letters A-F. Any number of the letters in the code may be the same. Possible codes are DABC, BBEA, CDDC, FEFF, and DDDD.

2. The code-breaker writes down his guess of the code, such BCED.

3. The code-maker indicates how close the guess is to the code with X's followed by O's. Each X indicates some letter in the guess which is the correct letter and in the correct position. Each O indicates some

letter in the guess which is the correct letter but in the wrong position. Only one letter in the guess can be matched with any one letter in the code. If the code is ECFF, a guess of BCED yields XO. A guess of EFEF yields XXO.

4. Continue steps 2 and 3 until the code is solved, a response of XXXX. Optional scoring is based on the number of guesses until solved.

## Variations

The game can be made more or less difficult by changing how many letters there are in the code and/or how far up the alphabet each letter can be.

To make the game more difficult the code-maker may be allowed to lie a specified number of times per game, such as exactly once.

A proprietary version of the game is sold under the name *MasterMind*. Colored pegs replace the letters.

## *Appendix VII:*
## *Strategy Board Games*

## 2-Person

- Dvonn

- Fanorona

- Halma

- Havannah

- Hex

- Poison Pot

- Pünct

- Realm

- Reversi/Othello

- Yinsch

- Zertz

## Multiple-Person

- Borderlands

- Chinatown

- Conquest

- Discretion

- El Grande

- Rail Baron

- Settlers of Catan

- Tikal

- Torres

- Vinci

- 1829

# *Appendix VIII:*
# *Lucid Dreaming*

There are many ways to encourage lucid dreaming. Next are some of the most common and basic ways. Elaborations of these, plus other approaches, are discussed in the first two resource books, particularly the second.

If you seldom remember dreams, it is useful to first spend some time developing this memory. Everyone dreams, but people differ in how often they recall their dreams after waking. Having the intent to remember is helpful. So as you fall asleep, have in mind the desire and intent to remember your dreams. Then, when you wake up after a dream, even briefly, immediately record your dream in a dream journal kept beside your bed. Don't wait to record, do it immediately after the dream. When you wake up in the morning, immediately record in detail all the dreams you can remember. Later, periodically go through your journal looking for common themes and images. Review and reflect on your journal entries before going to sleep.

One of the best ways to develop lucid dreaming is by asking yourself the question "Am I dreaming?" Do this many times throughout the day, particularly when you encounter something unusual or strange or when you encounter something similar to an image or symbol which comes up in your dream journal. Your awake answer to "Am I dreaming?" will be no, but be sure.

Eventually the mental habit of asking this question will carry over into the dream state. Then, when you ask "Am I dreaming?" the answer can be yes or maybe. At this point, look at your hands. If they do not look normal, such as being too small or having extra fingers, you are lucid dreaming. Another test is to look at a digital clock or writing, both of these change in unusual ways in dreams. Or, try to change the lighting in a dream, as with a light switch (it usually won't change). For your first few lucid dreams, don't try to alter the dream, simply maintain awareness. Later you can play with the dream and try to do something impossible, such as flying. (Just push off the ground.)

After having one or more lucid dreams, switch your pre-sleep intentions to having lucid dreams. That is, rather than going to sleep with the intent to remember dreams, have the intent to have a lucid dream. You might give yourself this suggestion several times before going to sleep.

Once you become proficient in lucid dreaming, you can fly wherever you want, have extraordinary senses and powers, call up anyone to interact with, put yourself in a learning situation, or eventually move on to dream yoga.

## Resources

Harary, Keith, and Pamela Weintraub. *Lucid Dreams in 30 Days.* St Martin's Press, 1989.

LaBerge, Stephen, and Howard Rheingold. *Exploring the World of Lucid Dreaming.* Ballantine Books, 1990.

Norbu, Namkhai. *Dream Yoga and the Practice of Natural Light.* Snow Lion, 2002.

Wangyal Tenzin. *The Tibetan Yogas of Dream and Sleep.* Snow Lion, 1998.

## Movies

The first movie contains discussions of the nature and practice of lucid dreaming. The rest of the films are based on the idea that what one takes to be "reality" is an artificially created "dream."

- *Waking Life*
- *The Matrix*
- *The Thirteenth Floor*
- *Total Recall*
- *Vanilla Sky*

# *Glossary*

## *advaita vedanta*

"Nondual end of the vedas," where the vedas are the earliest sacred works of Hinduism and yoga, and the vedanta is the end or conclusion of the vedas. It is an experiential understanding of the nonduality of reality; everything is interconnected. To the unawakened mind, reality appears to be composed of many separate parts; to the awakened mind, reality is nondual.

Shankara is the primary teacher of advaita vedanta, which is one of several schools of thought in vedanta. Some people describe the nondual in terms of God and how we become one with God, which was always the case. Others describe nonduality nontheistically, such as purely in terms of consciousness; nothing exists outside of consciousness, an aspect of the fundamental ground.

*See also* glossary entries "awakening" and "self-inquiry."

### attachment

The result of the mind clinging to certain contents of the mind, assumptions about self and reality, and personal frames of reference. Attachments may be to perceptions, rituals, expectancies, opinions, images of the self, or models of reality. Attachments cause resistance to change, distortions in perception and memory, impairment in thinking, and unwanted emotions.

As just described, this is the way the term "attachment" is used in yogic psychology and this manual. The meaning is similar to the term "addiction," but different than the psychodynamic use of "attachment," which refers to interpersonal bonding usually early in life.

See Resources, Level III: "Attachments."

## attitude

The mental set with which one approaches what one does, and thus is important in mental training. Attitude includes moods, associations, expectations, and intentions.

Optimal attitude usually includes acting with intention, persistent dedication, a welcoming openness to experience, a readiness to let go, being in the here and now, making friends with oneself, having fun, and not-doing.

*See also* glossary entry "not-doing."

## awakening

A popular metaphor for the process of personal/spiritual growth in which one disidentifies with the contents of the mind and moves into a broader conscious domain. It is similar to waking up from the sleep dream state and realizing that what one took for reality in the dream was just a construction of the mind.

For most people awakening seems to be a gradual process, facilitated by the practices described in this manual. Fundamentally, everyone is always already fully awake. Awakening involves discovering what is already true, outside of time and space; it is not acquiring something new in the future. It is an uncovering of the already present transpersonal level of being. Hence, partial or full awakening occurs any time.

See Resources, Level IV: "Awakening Practices," and Level V: "Awakened Mind." *See also* glossary entry "transpersonal."

### awareness

The behavior of the mind that involves simple and direct conscious observing of the contents and processes of the mind. It is just being aware; bare attention; detached observation; choiceless awareness. It is not thinking, judging, or categorizing; it is being aware of these mental processes.

Awareness has two basic attributes: breadth and clarity. A measure of awareness is in Appendix I.

### ayurveda

"Life knowledge," the natural healing system of India, developed over thousands of years. It involves working with nutrition, herbs, life force, color, massage, yoga, meditation, psychology, life style, spirituality, and surgery. One must deal with body, mind, and spirit.

See books by David Frawley and Vasant Lad, including Vasant Lad's *Textbook of Ayurveda* (The Ayurvedic Press, 2002).

### breathwork

Practices focusing on breathing as a way to improve the health of body/mind/spirit. Breathwork affects energy, relaxation, flow of the life force, and state of consciousness.

Hatha yoga includes practices to strengthen the lungs, remove phlegm, and wash out the nose. Pranayama, the yogic science of breath, includes exercises to alter the depth, duration, and frequency of breathing. Other pranayama practices involve eliminating or expanding the pause between inhalation and exhalation, and forcing unilateral nostril breathing.

See Resources, Level I: "Breathwork." *See also* glossary entries: life force, prana, pranayama, yoga.

### concentration

The learned control of the focus of one's attention. The behavior of the mind of keeping one's awareness, with varying degrees of one-pointedness, on a particular set of contents of the mind.

In Western psychology, concentration is a part of "attention." In Buddhist meditation, concentration is related to *shamatha,* "dwelling in tranquility." If a person sits quietly and practices a concentration form of meditation, the mind becomes calm and relaxed, which often relaxes the body.

Eventually concentration yields control of the contents of one's mind and the ability to disidentify with these contents and get distance from them. These effects facilitate psychological therapies, opening to new insights and awakening.

*See also* glossary entries: jhanas, meditation, and moment-to-moment concentration.

## drunken monkey

A metaphor for the untrained mind, commonly used in Asia. The mind is seen to be like a wild or drunken monkey that is running out of control. Sometimes the monkey is jumping from limb to limb in a tree. Sometimes the monkey is in a room with six windows corresponding to the five physical senses and the mental sense of thinking, remembering, and fantasizing. The monkey wildly runs from window to window.

A story tells of a monkey trap made from a gourd tied to a tree. Inside the hollowed-out gourd is monkey food. If the monkey reaches into the hole and grabs the food, it can't get its hand back out through the hole, and thus is caught. Of course, to be free, all the monkey has to do is let go of the food. This is a metaphor about attachments and the mind's clinging behavior.

## jhanas

Levels of absorption described in the classic yogic/Buddhist literature. In this literature there are two basic paths of awakening: the path of concentration/absorption and the path of awareness/insight.

Concentration leads to absorption, which leads to the jhanas. The jhanas go beyond the sensual to form, and then beyond form to the formless.

See Resources, Level V: "Jhanas."

## lateral thinking

A way to cultivate mental flexibility developed by Edward de Bono that emphasizes generating new ideas. In lateral thinking one may consider ideas that are wrong, illogical, impractical, or irrelevant to discover new, useful ideas.

Lateral thinking includes many different strategies, such as questioning assumptions, challenging categories and labels, and use of analogies. Lateral thinking helps one to escape rigid mental patterns and increase creativity and insight.

See Resources, Level I: "Mental Flexibility". *See also* glossary entry "PMI."

## life force

A basic vital energy whose presence separates the animate from the inanimate. The idea of a life force is found throughout the world. In Chinese it is called *chi* (or *qi*) and in Japanese *ki*. In Indian systems it takes many forms including prana and kundalini.

There are different suggestions about the source of this energy and the forms and paths it takes through the body. But nutrition and breathing are commonly held to be basic ways the universal energy is transmuted into forms for the body.

In traditional Asian healing systems, diseases are often related to this energy (e.g., inadequate, blocked, or unbalanced). Life force is affected by environmental factors, lifestyle, meditation, massage, acupuncture, and movement arts (e.g., tai chi, aikido, chi kung).

## meditation

"A family of self-regulation practices that focus on training attention and awareness in order to bring mental processes under greater voluntary control and thereby foster general mental well-being and development and/or specific capacities such as calm, clarity, and concentration" (Roger Walsh).

Although there is no agreement about a definition of "meditation," there is agreement on two points among all the major world's meditation traditions: (1) "Meditation" does not include thinking or daydreaming, although the term is often this way. One can meditate on one's thinking, but the thinking is not meditation. (2) All meditation involves the cultivation of concentration and/or awareness, as these terms and practices are described in this manual.

The object of meditation determines whether the practice is for creativity, mental exploration, physical healing, psychotherapy, personal/spiritual growth, religious practice, or something else. Meditation is usually not religious or occult.

See Resources, Level III: "Meditation."

## mindfulness

A Buddhist term for awareness, the fundamental practice of Buddhism. Although ultimately mindfulness means awareness, the cultivation of mindfulness is a blend of awareness training, concentration training, and attitude, as described in this book. Hence, definitions of mindfulness often combine and/or conflate awareness, concentration, and attitude.

Sometimes in Buddhist literature mindfulness refers to a property of the mind, and sometimes it refers to the cultivation of this property.

Also see the online article "Mindfulness: Significant Common Confusions" at www.uwf.edu/wmikulas/papers.

## moment-to-moment concentration (mtmc)

Precise one-pointed focus on whatever the mind is attending to, even as the mind moves from one object to another. This is in contrast to the one-pointed focus when the mind stays with one object of concentration, as is common in early concentration training.

## not-doing

Not adding an unnecessary heaviness or melodrama to what one is doing, getting one's limited self out of the way, and allowing the situation to spontaneously bring forth the appropriate action.

Similar to wu wei, the central practice of Taoism, not-doing can also be found in advaita vedanta, Zen, and some of the highest teachings in Tibetan Buddhism (dzogchen, mahamudra).

Also see article "not-doing." (Google "Mikulas not-doing" or go to uwf.edu/wmikulas/papers).

### pmi

A thinking tool, developed by de Bono, which stands for plus, minus, and interesting. When making a decision these categories are used to generate points of consideration of different choices.

*See also* glossary entry "lateral thinking."

### prana

A form of the life force, associated with the breath, that feeds all the organs of the body. A central component of Indian health systems, including yoga and ayurveda.

In Hinduism "prana" often refers to the universal life force. A distinction is sometimes made between this universal prana and the individual prana described in the previous paragraph.

*See also* glossary entries: ayurveda, life-force, pranayama, and yoga.

## pranayama

A set of procedures to purify, develop, strengthen, and redirect prana. The yogic science of breath, literally "breath control." The fourth limb of the eight limbs of yoga, as compiled by Patajali.

See Resources, Level III: "Pranayama."

## self-inquiry

The practice of mindfully looking for and at the experiential sense of self as subject, the entity that perceives, thinks, and acts. For example, right now as you are reading this, what is your direct immediate experience of some self that is doing the reading and thinking?

The primary practice of awakening taught by the yogi Ramana Maharshi. A doorway to the non-dual in advaita vedanta. A recurring meditation while on the vipassana path of insight.

See Resources, Level IV: "Self as Subject."

## transpersonal level

The domain of being that is superordinate to and/or prior to the self-centered personal reality. It is how the individual ("personal") is embedded in that which is greater than the individual ("trans-" meaning "beyond"), which creates and supports the individual.

In Conjunctive Psychology, it is recognized that essentially all people exist at four totally interrelated levels of being: biological, behavioral, personal, and transpersonal. The biological level includes the state and predispositions of the body. The behavioral level refers to what a person does. The personal level includes the individual's conscious experiential senses of self, will, and reality. The transpersonal level, described in the previous paragraph, includes those forces that construct the personal reality and sense of self and will.

## *vipassana*

A systematized set of Buddhist practices for cultivating mindfulness. Clear seeing in new, varied, and extraordinary ways.

Vipassana meditation is often called "insight meditation" because the cultivation of mindfulness leads to a form of insight (*prajna*), which is an immediately experienced intuitive wisdom. This insight involves mindful and penetrating seeing into the fundamental nature of things in a way that transforms one's being.

See Resources, Level III: "Vipassana." *See also* glossary entries: awareness, meditation, and mindfulness.

## *yoga*

From the Sanskrit for "union" or "yoke," any practice that leads to the union of the individual self with the universal Self, transpersonal consciousness, or God. Although yoga is primarily associated with Hinduism and Buddhism, a practitioner of yoga may be of any tradition.

Different yogas stress different elements: Hatha yoga stresses physical discipline, postures, and breathwork, ideally as a preparation for meditation. Bhakti yoga stresses love and devotion. Karma yoga stresses selfless service. And jhana yoga stresses knowledge and discriminating wisdom.

# Meditation

## For Beginners

Techniques for Awareness, Mindfulness & Relaxation

STEPHANIE CLEMENT, Ph.D.

## Meditation for Beginners
*Techniques for Awareness, Mindfulness & Relaxation*
STEPHANIE CLEMENT, PH.D.

Break the barrier between your conscious and unconscious minds.

Perhaps the greatest boundary we set for ourselves is the one between the conscious and less conscious parts of our own minds. We all need a way to gain deeper understanding of what goes on inside our minds when we are awake, asleep, or just not paying attention. Meditation is one way to pay attention long enough to find out.

*Meditation for Beginners* explores many different ways to meditate—including kundalini yoga, walking meditation, dream meditation, tarot meditations, and healing meditation—and offers a step-by-step approach to meditation, with exercises that introduce you to the rich possibilities of this age-old spiritual practice. Improve concentration, relax your body quickly and easily, work with your natural healing ability, and enhance performance in sports and other activities. Just a few minutes each day is all that's needed.

**978-0-7387-0203-2, 264 pp., 5 ³⁄₁₆ x 8**       **$13.95**

---

# Meditation for Your Life
### *Creating a Plan that Suits Your Style*
### ROBERT BUTERA, PHD

Engage in the process of self-inquiry and understanding with expert teacher Robert Butera. All meditation methods are valid forms of practice, but they don't fit everyone alike. *Meditation for Your Life* explains the six basic forms and guides readers in identifying which ones suit them best. Questions and answers, exercises, and journaling engage readers in learning what steps they can take to make meditation (and its benefits) an enduring part of their lives. Wellness and inner calm are achievable goals with suitable meditation styles—using techniques of breathwork or visualization, mantra or devotion, mindfulness or contemplation. Includes special emphasis on overcoming frequent blocks to inner growth.

**978-0-7387-3414-9, 312 pp., 6 x 9**                     **$16.99**

---

# MEDITATION

*as*

## SPIRITUAL PRACTICE

GENEVIEVE L. PAULSON

## Meditation as Spiritual Practice
### Genevieve L. Paulson

Meditation has many purposes: healing, past life awareness, mental clarity, and relaxation. This practice can also enhance our spiritual lives by bringing about "peak experiences" or transcendental states. *Meditation as Spiritual Practice* focuses on the practice of meditation for expanding consciousness and awareness. The techniques in this treasured guidebook can also help one in developing clairvoyance, clairaudience, and other psychic abilities.

**978-0-7387-0851-5, 224 pp., 6 x 9**                    **$14.95**

---